DECORATED MAN

Tiwa Indian. New Mexico

Editor: Joanne Greenspun
Designer: Gerald Pryor

Library of Congress Cataloging in Publication Data

Virel, André.
    Decorated man.

    Translation of Corps en fête.
    1. Body-marking. 2. Cosmetics. 3. Beauty,
Personal. I. Title.
    GN419.15.V5713 1980 391'.65   79-14467

Library of Congress Catalog Card Number: 79-14467

© 1979 Draeger Editeur, Paris
Published in 1980 by Harry N. Abrams, Incorporated, New York
All rights reserved. No part of the contents of this book may be
reproduced without the written permission of the publishers

Printed and bound in France

DECORATED MAN

THE HUMAN BODY AS ART

Text by André Virel
Photographs by Charles and Josette Lenars
Translated from the French by I. Mark Paris

Harry N. Abrams, Inc., Publishers, New York

Contents

WITHDRAWN

Introduction

When man dreams of being naked and free, he recaptures his childhood and innocence. To take off one's clothes is to strip oneself not only of personal history, but of History. It means going back to the very beginning and reliving one's birth outside of chronological time. The body is naked at the convulsive climax of uninhibited love. When our two skins touch, is it yours or mine that I feel? The body is naked, too, when it is involved in initiation rites. The etymology of the word reminds us that "initiation" is actually a return to the beginning, a new birth. And though we dress the bodies of deceased persons for funerals, time will cause the finery to fade and the garments of flesh to disintegrate, leaving a hard, white skeleton that is even more naked than the naked body when it was alive. Thus, there is an intimate relationship between nudity and the three great acts of life, be they considered events or symbols: birth, love, and death.

For modern man, nudity is the adversary of clothing. Nudity means freedom, whereas clothing has a social connotation. If clothing turns into finery, it is because we are celebrating: special dress for special occasions. But for primitive man, whose dress is often reduced to bare essentials, the more rudimentary the clothing, the more nudity and adornment arouse, stimulate, and complement each other. Through such artificial means as tattooing, scarification, and body painting, naked skin becomes a living ornament. In those civilizations that have maintained direct and permanent contact with nature, the combination of naked skin and adornment accompanies, commemorates, or simply suggests birth, love, and death. Newborn babies, men and women toiling day after day, engaged couples, circumcised boys, excised girls, dancers—we always see their naked bodies as *celebrating* bodies. That is why pictures of these "naked peoples"—to use Max-Pol Fouchet's lovely phrase—make up such a large part of the illustrations selected for this book. That is also why we have been careful to let the pictures interact freely according to their similarities or differences, and why we have been just as careful not to arrange them in a didactic, and therefore necessarily artificial, manner. Four frames of reference, however, have been chosen: Seduction, Threat, Caste, and Ritual.

Whether our wish be to appear or disappear, captivate or terrify, we feel compelled to transform our appearance by "sloughing our skin," at least for others. Where does it come from, the skin that is both the subject and object of this metamorphosis? Our knowledge about its formation casts a surrealistic glow on the origin and subsequent adventure of our bodies. Let us watch the miracle as it takes place.

The primordial sphere from which we are born, the ovum, moves. A rectilinear cleft appears on the enclosing membrane and widens. The now-separated areas on either side come to life and nearly break apart only to reunite and become absorbed into the organism. Now begins the real alchemy. From this ovular "skin" will emerge all superficial body growth (hair, nails, teeth, etc.), cutaneous glands, external sensory organs, and oral and anal mucous membranes. The outside of the "skin" will develop into the epidermis, while another part of the same integument folds itself in to form an internal groove, thus marking the first stage of an organ whose role will be to receive a picture of everything that surrounds us: the nervous system, the medium of our life as a process of communication. Thus, our skin—more than a square meter of surface separating us from the world, yet linking us to it through the sense of touch—and our nervous system have a common origin. This genesis prepares, structures, and establishes contact between man and his environment; through this communication, man universalizes his body and anthropomorphizes the universe. It is as if he placed himself at the center of the world; yet, at the same time, the world becomes rooted within him. From this

Young woman. Mt. Hagen, New Guinea

contact emerge imagination and consciousness. Such is the starting point of our advance through life, one which, by generating a world that it continually transforms, seems to be a complete reversal of causality.

Our skin is a mirror endowed with properties even more wonderful than those of a magic looking glass. The primeval mirror that envelops the ovum splits apart only to be swallowed up within itself. Then it reappears on the other side of the original fissure. This divided mirror that is the skin and nervous system combined thus ends up looking at itself, so to speak, resulting in a confrontation that stimulates a never-ending movement of images and the birth of what is aptly referred to as reflexive thought. Nonetheless, this is nothing more than a manner of speaking, a simplification of the way it happens in real life. How complacent we are when it comes to our own adult psyche, which loves above all to be reassured!

The skin is a two-sided mirror that does triple duty. Its outer surface reflects not only the world we call objective reality, but the living world within the body. Its inner surface reflects the outside world in a way that communicates it to the shifting night of cells that fills our organs. Our skin, therefore, receives not only signals that come to us from our environment and relays them to centers of the nervous system for deciphering, but signals from the world within, which are then translated into quantifiable terms. A specialist in this field, Paul Blum, writes that the skin is "the mirror of an organism's functioning"; for its moistness or dryness, odor, texture, and all its other aspects are so many symptoms that enable us to form diagnoses. As the mirror of our passions and feelings, the skin trembles with love or fear. Its electrical resistance varies with our emotions. It has been suggested that electrodermal response to stimuli may be considered a barometer of our alertness, which increases or decreases depending on our emotional condition at the time. One can see how dangerous such knowledge could be if improperly used by the police: if submitted to an electronic lie-detector test, we could be betrayed by our own skin!

Even more manifest is the living mirror—call it a trap or a blank page—we hold out to the world. When the body celebrates, it shimmers with the reflections of forests, lakes, and prairies. It quivers with feathers or the fine, thick hair of fur-bearing animals. Anything in the universe, when placed on the skin, becomes adornment: Polynesian flowers, iguana skins, claws, the teeth of sea creatures, shells. Gold and brass compete in brilliance with turquoise, coral, mother-of-pearl, blue and bronze-colored Coleoptera, fiery seeds, russet fibers, raffias, and pearls! Let us not forget the preferred jewel of primitive finery, the cowrie, a split shell that is curiously reminiscent of the aforementioned ovum. There are headdresses, necklaces, and earrings sometimes so heavy that they tear the wearer's earlobes. Adornment is at once nature made man and man made nature. Thus, everyone is capable of restraining gods, bewitching animals, charming plants—and seducing one's fellowman.

To decorate the skin, apply makeup to it, dress it in feathers, shells, and flowers, or make radical changes in its natural appearance—these habits are as familiar to a Papuan as to a Hollywood star. But are they peculiar to the human species? It's rather doubtful, given a number of observable phenomena in the animal and plant kingdoms that are included under the vague but suggestive rubric "mimicry."

The minnow is gray against the sandy gray background of a lake, but turns a darker color when it swims over a background of black rocks or brown algae. This is a classic case of animal camouflage, a phenomenon with which naturalists are quite familiar. Although there are many such examples, we shall mention only the modest, graceful cousin of the bullfrog, the tree frog: the emerald green it wears in foliage or grassy meadows turns reddish as soon as it alights on the trunk of a tree.

A methodical mind would undoubtedly perceive two possible motivations for this behavior. The first would be a wish to disappear, to blend in with the anonymity of natural surroundings. The second would be the wish to creep up on one's prey without warning. Such is the case with the leopard men, to mention but one example in our species. In either case, however, the technique is the same: the prey camouflages itself to avoid being seen by the predator, and the predator takes on the appearance of its prey so as not to alarm it. Thus, there are probably two fundamental kinds of mimicry—offensive and defensive—each of which makes use of the same camouflage techniques for contrary purposes.

Actually, mimicry is but one of many mechanisms that occur in nature, for living things seek not only to hide under the protective cover of anonymity, but to entice or threaten. And, at times, the line separating seduction and threat is a fine one indeed. Certain female glowworms emit a luminous signal that attracts males for mating. But the same luminous signal attracts the males of different species, who respond to the same invitation only to end up being devoured.

In the case of mimicry, however, illusion is the absolute rule. It's a question of life or death. There are species that wear sumptuous patterns and dazzling colors for the sole purpose of giving themselves a frightening appearance. Thus the ocelli of certain nocturnal butterflies would be designed to terrify small birds that mistake them for the eyes of birds of prey. Beauty can spell menace and death as well as offer the promise of life and happiness.

Mimicry of form (the stick insect and leaf insect are but two cases in point); mimicry of color, the play of light, shading, and material such as one sees in painting; mimicry of pattern (stripes, spots, speckles, ocelli)—the variations on the theme of appearance and reality are endless. Yet, mimicry is far from universal or invariable. The American hamster is pale in sandy regions and dark in volcanic regions. But would the light- and dark-colored hamsters be able to change colors if they were to exchange territories?

At the same time, mimicry is not always so closely related to a given species' habitat; it might vary according to the cycle of the seasons. The ptarmigan's feathers are white in winter and reddish in summer, as are the coats of the ermine and the Arctic fox. We should also bear in mind that mimicry is not necessarily a survival mechanism, for countless species have managed to live without it. There are strong, robust species which, far from attempting to conceal themselves, fairly cry out with savage, arrogant displays of color. For example, dark fur and a crown of antlers make the reindeer especially noticeable against fields of snow. In addition, some animals see only in black and white; while others, though unable to perceive certain colors of the spectrum, are capable of seeing others we humans cannot. Bees, for instance, are sensitive to ultraviolet light. There are also more subtle forms of camouflage that one could refer to as second-degree mimicry. Some animals alter their appearance by taking on precisely the color or shade that cannot be perceived by their enemies. It all takes place as if the prey had an exact knowledge of the capabilities and limitations of the eyes that watch them. Knowledge? Intuition? Instinct? How can we explain this miracle of nature, by which the mirror can vary its reflections according to how it is presumably being observed?

When seen from above, several species of fish have a coloring that matches the dark shades of the ocean depths; but when seen from below, they wear lighter colors that blend in with the brighter surface of the water. In this instance, the back and belly of the fish are negative reflections of the environment either faces: the scales that "look at" the light are dark, while those facing the darkness of the deep are light.

Chance or life's "design"? The frequency of such occurrences makes it tempting to believe that design has something to do with it. Can we attribute to mere chance the fact that, when attacked, a Cephalopod squirts out a black cloud that is as dark as its own body? While the predator is busy attacking this decoy, the real prey escapes by turning completely white. Can we even be so sure that, unlike man, who can devise his own camouflage techniques, animals capable of mimicry use no other tool but their bodies? The distinction between human invention and natural mechanism is not always as clear-cut as we would like to believe. For example, there is a crab that conceals itself as it moves about by covering its rough shell with plant debris torn from the algae that grow in its environment. But place it among plants that differ in form and color from those of the first habitat, and it immediately sloughs off the old, now-useless camouflage and dons new clothing borrowed from its new surroundings. This crab changes "masks" to fit the circumstances; a being endowed with reason would probably act no differently.

The mask can be found among a large number of primitive peoples still in existence today, but does that necessarily mean that it is the exclusive property of man? Could it be considered one of the hallmarks of our species? Whether dreaded or desired, sacred or accursed, god or devil, seductive or threatening, masks defy neat, definitive classification by confronting us with vexing questions that throw our habits into disarray. What does the celebrated mask of the *inconnue de la Seine* have to do with, say, the mask worn by His Majesty King Carnival? The former harks back to myths that tell how a river restored the uninjured, unadulterated body of Ophelia or the tender, but forever nameless face of Sleeping Beauty. The other mask—we can still see it in Nice or Rio—refers to the grotesque figure of a madman decked out in a king's crown, embodiment of the annual, short-lived transformation of profane everyday life into something sacred. One begins to wonder if one of the essential characteristics common to all masks isn't their ambivalence or ambiguity, and that ambivalence and ambiguity are what control the genre and lay down the rules of the game. If such is indeed the case, then the mask may be looked upon as the undisputed leader in "two-facedness," the intermediary *par excellence* that ensures movement between two opposing values. Fraught with mystery, masks set us dreaming and push us into the labyrinth of that other life that fills us with the rapture of being lost. Whenever I pause for a moment to listen to the voice of the mask, I hear the echo of an echo, for I am reminded of a schizophrenic woman I once met.

Eighteen years old, she was a tall, skinny girl suffering from anorexia. She seemed to glide over the ground. She wore an intent gaze as she walked in. Rarely has a patient's first visit made such an indelible impression on me. Her pale face was so caked with makeup that it no longer had any semblance of life in it; but it wasn't the face of a statue or a dead person, either. The purple circles around her sparkling eyes, the pronounced black eyebrows, the shading around those prominent cheekbones that looked as if they had been whitened with chalk—everything seemed to say: no, I am neither death nor life, but fleeting death! Upon entering my office, she bent her head and turned away. I found out the reason afterward: her eyes had lighted on my mirror. Later on, this schizophrenic informed me that she could look at herself in a mirror without ever seeing her reflection. She claimed that, by painting a mask on her face, she had found a way of making herself invisible to her own eyes.

Where does the word "mask" come from? The French word *masque* is derived from the Italian *maschera,* which itself evolved from a root of unknown origin, *mask* ("black"). *Masque* can also be traced back to a modern Provençal term used to refer to a saucy girl or woman. Thus, *masque* has two different origins and meanings. Its ambivalence in Provençal is also worth noting. We have mentioned that it is roughly the equivalent of minx or hussy; but it is also the origin of *mascotte,* an appealing word that carries a contrary meaning, lucky charm.

The mask covers the face that is the very image of our person. Now, where does the word "person" come from? From *persona,* an Etruscan word that refers to either a character in a play or the mask worn by the actor portraying the character. That is, the thing that hides (the mask) and the thing hidden (the person) are denoted by terms that are different in origin but identical in meaning. And isn't the French word *personne* just as ambivalent? As a synonym of both "someone" and "anyone," it can refer to a human being irrespective of sex as well as the absence or negation of that human being. *Je n'y suis pour personne* means "I'm not on anyone's side," that is, for no human being. The word has a peculiar ring to it in the following text written by Jean Piveteau, a paleontologist: "If a wayfarer had been miraculously transported to our planet during that not-so-distant era (one or two million years back), he could have traveled the world over without meeting anyone *(sans rencontrer personne).* I repeat, without meeting anyone. Let us try to fully appreciate the sense of strangeness, alienation, and loneliness that those words convey."

Of course, we cannot imagine a world without anyone, because to imagine it is to place ourselves in the world to begin with. But we *can* imagine traveling about without meeting anyone. Could it have been this inescapable loneliness that gave birth to the mask? Could the mask—whether the primitive masks of old or of today—be considered the prototype mediator between man and the world? As always, it's much more complex than that, and we would be running a strong risk of self-deception if we were to look upon the mask as nothing more than a mediator between the profane that is always "self" and the sacred that is always everything else. It is because the self dissolves, because the masked self not only possesses but is possessed by a god, that the mask "I" am wearing is that of a god or devil—or more precisely, of the All that is both god *and* devil, sickness *and* health. Which is tantamount to saying that the masked All makes itself visible to me as a phase or aspect of my own image. Thus, the revelation experienced by initiates during rites of passage consists of just such an "unmasking." Once allowed to share in the Great Secret, they know that such and such a *personne* breathes life into such and such a mask.

In order to personalize our distant forbears, we resort to the epithets *faber, erectus,* and *sapiens.* However, as Vercors reminds us in *Les Animaux dénaturés,* it is only because *homo* is the *faber* of amulets that he is *erectus* and *sapiens.* This might be seen as proof that he possesses a sixth sense, the sense of sacredness. Which is, once again, both true and false; for this sixth sense is the sense of profaneness as well as sacredness. It is, in other words, nothing more than the sense of their inevitable ambivalence. With this as our premise, we could talk in terms of a *homo persona* whose adventure was destined to be the long, but ahistorical adventure of the mask.

Before they ended up imitating the human form—although, granted, animal features were sometimes added—masks were probably purely animal in appearance, a perfect mimicry used by the hunter to approach his prey. And before that? The mask might have consisted of a face daubed with plants, a raw, natural thing resembling nothing but itself, unrelated to anything that preceded it. Now, we could devise an ontology of the mask that would yield a fairly close copy of a phylogenic model. But we must remember that evolution grows like a bush and that it is our own complacency and need for convenience that induce us to set up neat, linear patterns of development. In point of fact, an oversimplified scheme of this sort would be covered with countless growths branching out from the trunk. We could talk in terms of the genetics of the mask, but not the history. Or we could, at the very most, conceive of the mask as a sum total of stages in an evolution: but here again, we are dealing with paleontology, not history. It's like those convertible masks whose hinges enable the wearer to effect several transformations by a series of disclosures—a catfish opens up to reveal a crow which, in turn, opens up to reveal a man—thereby "achieving evolution not only in thought but in deed," to quote André Breton.

"The very act of listing and examining our discoveries," wrote André Malraux, "frustrates our search for the historical common denominator of Negro art and indeed of all primitive art, including that of children and madmen. On the other hand, one underlying similarity does stand out: they all lie outside of history, outside of chronological time." And when Malraux adds that "primitive art has no architecture," he expresses an idea that we put differently elsewhere in this text, namely, that these art forms exist, not in the four-dimensional chronological world of three-dimensional space, but the three-dimensional chronic world of two-dimensional space. Though the latter world has fewer dimensions, its possibilities are no less infinite. To illustrate primitive art's inexhaustible generative capacity, Malraux cites certain voodoo sculptures still made in Dahomey and which, in his words, "appear only among the dead."

Man was born when he began to question. Masks were born when man became the object of his own questioning. Thus, the mask is the primordial reminder of our role as symbols; it makes a hole in time the same way a tooth is broken during certain rites of passage. And what kind of answers does it provide? Wonder, amazement, forgotten thoughts, rediscovered experiences, fusion, trance, dance, dizziness, escape from the self through living death, exposed skin turned inside out like a glove. True, memory has the power to reactivate all history, even prehistory. But the mask looms out with a cry of primal oblivion and triumphant remembrance by catalyzing a real metaphysical confrontation between "sameness" and "otherness."

While taking part in various African rituals and celebrations, I was once mistaken for a target by some masked dancers who were rushing toward me as if about to attack. I rooted my feet to the spot and stood firm so as not to retreat, for such was the nature of the game—to rivet one's eyes to the deep, black sockets of the mask. At the very last minute, the masks came to a dead stop. Though a collision was averted, I could feel the violent breath of the dancers brush against my face. Was I afraid? I dare say I was, but it was an exhilarating fear, the kind experienced at the critical moment of a battle or during the final seconds of a happy death. For a fleeting instant, I thought I was that mask.

How could History possibly give masks meaning, since every mask is a narrow escape from History? That is why our historical era is witnessing the death of the mask. It is an unusual thing these days for all clocks to be momentarily stilled by this intruding messenger of utopia. Masks appear to have vanished at a very early stage of all great historical civilizations. That is to say, the mask underwent a metamorphosis that turned it into the immutable golden ornament that covered the Pharaoh's face during his voyage to the next life. Just the same, there is speculation as to whether the mask simply took on a mask of its own, whether it was still extant in ancient Egypt.

What are those animal-headed figures we see marching across stelae, frescos, and paintings in Egyptian temples and tombs? Masks? Perhaps not as the word was used to describe the famous Paleolithic "sorcerer" that was as much a product of a prehistorian's imagination as of the Trois Frères cave in Ariège, France. These figures were no longer "manimals," but gods in the shape of "manimals." No more were divine faces covered by masks; now the very face of the god was a living mask. Gods became incarnate and masks became flesh. As man progressed toward individuation and ever-increasing socialization, he exchanged his collective identification with animals for a personal identification with himself. Above the crowd of part-human, part-animal gods that can be found from one end of Egypt to the other stands the sphinx, a "manimal" in reverse with a human head attached to a lion's body. And there is Osiris, the first god-turned-man, the first man-god, who was depicted with purely human features. He was destined to be dismembered and then reconstructed to form a synthesis of all-inclusive animality and the unified territory of Egypt. Osiris marked the invention of a puzzle that was at once body, collectivity, and geography.

In Europe, the mask survived as more than just an appurtenance of certain folklores. It got a new lease on life from theater, not just the theater *per se* but also the street theater that is Carnival or Mardi Gras. This should come as no surprise. Granted, theater has its roots in sacred traditions; but beyond the church square lay the profane wilderness that was the temple's counterpart—the street. Of course, the mask did end up parodying itself. It seemed to waive its prerogatives by shrinking to the size of the person who wore it. It became nothing more than a passport to fashionable anonymity. But there were also times when, at the height of the festivities, it could evoke once again the name and magic of a velvety-pawed animal from the distant past: the French called the black velvet mask that women once wore to masked balls *un loup* ("wolf"). There were even times when it could cause History to shudder with primordial terror. It was at such moments that the mask reassumed the status of living enigma it had never really lost. And so it happened...

"On Thursday, September 18, 1698, at three o'clock in the afternoon, M. de Saint-Mars, commanding officer of the Bastille, arrived from the islands of Sainte Marguerite and Saint Honorat. He had brought with him in his litter a prisoner formerly kept at Pinerol, name unknown, who is kept masked at all times. He was put in the Bazinière Tower, where he remained until nightfall, at which time I myself led him, at nine o'clock, to a room in the Bertaudière Tower, which M. de Saint-Mars had ordered me to have completely furnished before his arrival..." These lines are taken from the journal kept by the king's lieutenant, Etienne du Jonca. Five years later, in the same journal, we read: "The prisoner whose identity was still concealed behind a black velvet mask, and who had been feeling somewhat more ill while leaving mass, died at ten o'clock at night without any major illness. He was buried on Tuesday, November 20, at four o'clock in the afternoon, in the cemetery of our parish, St. Paul's. His burial cost forty *livres*.... The prisoner had been kept in the Bastille for five years and sixty-two days, not counting the day of his burial..."

This strange prisoner crops up again in the papers of the fortress's former commanding officer: "Names and occupations of prisoners: prisoner formerly at Pinerol, forced to wear a black velvet mask at all times. Name and occupation never determined. Reason for imprisonment: never determined."

It is believed that the burial certificate drawn up by Vicar Poitevin of St. Paul's parish and signed by M. de Rosarges, adjutant of the Bastille, and M. Reilhe, surgeon of the fortress, is a false document. It assigns the prisoner the name of Marchioly and puts his age at forty-five, even though he was actually over sixty years old. It is also believed that Voltaire knew the truth but would not have dared reveal it except in a veiled and incomplete way. At the age of nineteen, the prisoner is thought to have learned the secret of his birth by forcing open a casket in which his guardian, M. de Saint-Mars, kept his personal papers. It was after this discovery that he was locked up and never allowed to appear without a mask. Who was he really? The Duke of Beaufort? The Duke of Monmouth? The Count of Vermandois, illegitimate son of Louis XIV and Louise de La Vallière? Avedick, the Patriarch of Armenia? The fact that he was the object of so much precaution, expense, surveillance, and respect, those many years of safeguarded anonymity, the falsification of his death certificate—everything points to this being a case where the truth is more legend than anything else. The man without a face or identity may have been, in fact, the twin brother of the Sun King, a title bestowed on Louis XIV after he was seen wearing a golden mask at a masquerade. Now *there* was something to captivate and inspire the author of *The Three Musketeers*! But the mystery of the prisoner in the Bastille summons up something quite different from a velvet mask, something confining, hard, impenetrable, inviolable—an iron mask. Popular legend has it that the prisoner from the Lerins Islands wore just such a mask.

It is believed that this sinister masked man—the living antithesis of the Sun King—was born on September 16, 1638, and died at the age of sixty-five on Monday, November 19, 1703, or nearly twelve years before the death of his supposed twin brother, Louis XIV. One might well look upon his story as a real-life counterpart of Gérard de Nerval's tale, "Le Roi de Bicêtre," except that, if we consider our mystery man against the backdrop of History, fact turns out to be stranger than fiction. *The year of his death marked the beginning of the Sun King's decline.* Beyond the French frontier, there was the betrayal of Savoy and Portugal's alliance with the English, who, for their part, were soon to seize Gibraltar. On the domestic front, the Huguenots were in revolt from Lozère to Gard. It was then that the Englishman, the Duke of Marlborough ("Marlborough s'en va-t-en guerre, mironton, mironton, mirontaine") formed an alliance with the Austrians to drive the French out of Germany and the Low Countries. In northern Italy, the grandson of Henri IV, Maréchal Vendôme, began his attack on Verrua—a town whose defenses consisted of twenty-three cannonballs—located northeast of Turin at the junction of the Po and Dora Baltea rivers. The siege of this small fortified town lasted six months and five days, and it spelled the approaching end of Louis XIV's conquests. Curiously enough, the very same turning point in the glory of France was tied in to another incident involving masks. Here is how Saint-Simon reports it in his *Mémoires*:

"Lieutenant General Bouligneux and Brigadier Wartigny were killed at Verrua: two men of real ability, but quite remarkable for other reasons as well. The previous winter, several lifelike wax masks of court figures had been made, but they were worn beneath other masks in such a way that, when the first mask was removed, one would be fooled into mistaking the second mask for the wearer's face when all the time his real face would be underneath. This jest was a source of great amusement. When winter came round this year, people wanted to have some more fun with them. To everyone's great surprise, all of these lifelike masks were found to be as fresh as when they had been put away after Carnival, *except* for those of Bouligneux and Wartigny, which, though still perfect likenesses of the two men, had become pale and drawn the way people's faces do just after death. They showed up that way at a masked ball and created such horror that they tried to freshen them with rouge; but the color faded as soon as it was applied, and the haggard features could not be corrected. This struck me as being so extraordinary that I thought it worth relating here. But I should have refrained from doing so had not, in addition to myself, the entire court been the astonished witnesses of this peculiarity, not just once but on several occasions. Finally, the two masks were thrown away."

As Roger Caillois points out, "Masks provided entertainment for the French court around 1700, for they lent themselves to amusing ambiguities. But when masks make an unexpected and unsettling appearance in the chronicles of a writer as down-to-earth as Saint-Simon, they create a disconcertingly uncanny effect worthy of E. T. A. Hoffmann or Edgar Allan Poe."

We mentioned before that History cannot give the mask *meaning*. However, under certain unusual or bizarre circumstances, the mask can give this or that historical episode mythological *significance*. A story can be related only after the occurrence of some mythical event. Every god that descends to earth is, by definition, the inventor of a calendar. Conversely, there is always a mask ready to fulfill its eternal, ahistorical mission of stopping the clock, breaking the flow of time, and taking us back to the very beginning.

Today, the reign of the mask-turned-flesh is coming to an end. Its only progeny is the human head-turned-mask. It was that choreographer of language, Jacques Prévert, who drew up a list of these heads in a 1931 text entitled "Attempted Description of a Dinner of Heads in Paris, France":

"Those reverently...
"Those heartily...
"Those tricoloring...
"Those dedicating...
"Those believing...
"Those believing they believe...
"Those running, flying, and avenging us, all of them, and many others were proudly entering the Elysée Palace, gravel crunching beneath their feet, and all of them were jostling one another and rushing about because there was a big dinner of heads and everyone had one made to order. One of them had the head of a clay pipe, another, an English admiral's head. There were stink-bomb heads, Galliffet heads, heads of animals sick in the head, Auguste Comte heads, Rouget de Lisle heads, St. Theresa heads, headcheese heads, foot heads, His Eminence heads, and dairymen heads..."

As we can see, gone are the days when man identified himself with the animal he was hunting; now he identified himself with the hunted animal. It's the age of "those covering their faces with a *loup* (mask or wolf) in order to eat lamb." Jacques Prévert orchestrates a striking and fascinating ballet of masks both monstrous and sacred. It is the ballet of History's masks. The setting is the Elysée Palace, but the Kremlin or the White House would do just as well. All of a sudden, farce turns into tragedy; everyone begins to tremble. The roles reverse. Now it's History's turn to barge in on the cardboard heads:

"...A man with a man's head walked in, a man whom no one had invited and who gently placed a basket containing the head of Louis XVI on the table. Unspeakable horror gripped the room: teeth chattered, old men croaked, and doors clattered with fear. We're done for; we've beheaded a locksmith..."

What could be stranger than a man with a man's head walking into a masked world! Or more reckless! Here is how the description of this dinner of heads ends. "A carafe flung from afar by an indignant pigeon-fancier hits the man smack in the forehead as he is talking about how much he loves to laugh. He falls down; the Pigeon-Soldier has been avenged. The official cardboard cutouts trample him to death with their feet."

The odd and disturbing thing is that the basket-bearer remains nameless. Scandalmongers claim that this man is a society, perhaps even all of society. Let's welcome him with open arms. But the man is dead and History hesitates. Is it because he was sacrificed so unceremoniously? The sacrifice of this nobody cannot be dismissed as a mere incident. Music!... the dance resumes. It's the fourteenth of July. Soldiers file past to the great delight of civilians on leave. They don't know whether it's Easter or New Year's. St. John is taken for the summer solstice and Jesus for the Egyptian god Horus, who in his day was already being taken for the winter solstice, the dying sun that is the harbinger of the coming spring. But what does History matter! It's a holiday and we're twenty years old again.

Seduction

Makeup used by women today, temporary markings crudely painted on the bare skin, indelible tattoos, primitive masks worn by men, modern velvet masks worn by men and women alike—all adornment induces human beings to be something other than themselves. A wish to vanish from sight, but at the same time to exist. In hopes of being noticed. As oneself? As someone dressed up? In this manner, a personality dons a persona and, in the process, runs the risk of being, not noticed, but misunderstood. Just the same, when someone takes notice of the real "me," he looks for an ego that the very act of being noticed might help *me* see and bring to life. How deep and wide is the chasm between involuntary and deliberate seduction, between the act of being seductive and the act of seducing! Is the gulf separating love and possession just as deep?

Men and women attract, charm, enthrall, captivate, and bewitch each other. Either is capable of seducing to the point of fascinating, spellbinding, killing, or leading the other astray. The shades of difference between seducing and casting spells are endless. The latter means to do whatever is necessary so that another person becomes "possessed," that is, a victim of a devil's physical or emotional assaults. Every spell involves a wish to make the other person belong to you body and soul. In *every* case, the person doing the bewitching turns the victim into his chattel. Thus, casting spells means identifying oneself with a devil: to *be* in order to *have*. What appears to be not only the most harmless, but indeed most delightful, act of all—seduction—actually contains the seeds of everything that is most diabolical about bewitchment.

Seduction can bring either the body, or language, or both into play: it is theater. Make reality your stage, and seduction takes the form of "real-life" body language.

This word-made-flesh can utter cries for help through fits of hysteria, fainting spells, cataleptic ecstasy, and trances. Seduction can become dreaming incarnate. As mediator between the subject and the real world, imagination has the power to cause stigmata to appear or a certain area of the senses to become anesthetized. Religious conversion, for example, can bring on a somatization that comes about, as Freud put it, "in collusion with the body." The Middle Ages called it possession. How many witches were burned at the stake for wearing the signature of their pact with the devil on their skin! Individuals possessed by evil spirits were referred to as energumens and were hunted down because people imputed to them terrible powers or, at other times, harmless but very strange knowledge. Such was the case with the possessed individual who, according to statements made by both the famous Protestant surgeon Ambroise Paré and Jean Fernel, physician to Henri II, spoke Greek and Latin without ever having learned these languages!

Sometimes the devil won out. During the seventeenth century, for instance, the Church was seduced by Sister Jeanne des Anges, a nun whose hysterical fits eventually led Urbain Grandier, the priest of Loudun, to the rack and the stake.

To be possessed by the devil means to be held so completely in his grasp that he can influence the victim's actions. Possession turns the energumen into a witch despite himself; he proceeds to channel his energy toward spellbinding, bewitching, and possessing others. Perhaps we shall find the key to understanding possession as it occurred in medieval or primitive societies if we turn to its counterpart in modern society—hysteria.

There are, in fact, undeniable similarities between the symptoms of hysteria as described by psychiatry and certain states, either spontaneous or induced, observed by ethnologists among primitive peoples. There are also similarities between the exorcisms performed by shamans and medicine men on the one hand, and, on the other, certain techniques popular among therapists today. In either case, the symptoms consist of monotonous chanting conducive to a hypnotic state or, at least, a lowered state of alertness and the use of mental images as a means of increasing symbolic capacity.

Here is how Thérèse Lempérière describes the hysterical personality: "Everything is geared to attracting attention, pleasing, and seducing. There is nothing the hysteric fears more than going unnoticed, and this need to make an appearance brings into play devices and stratagems usually associated with the theater. Making scenes, role-playing, and other theatrics are the hysteric's ways of fulfilling the irresistible compulsion to avert genuine encounters with other people. The hysteric's true self resists self-disclosure by hiding behind disguises and donning the masks of various characters. Unable to concoct a life story on a genuinely personal level or an identity that it can call its own, the hysterical personality is induced to live vicariously through other people...."

A hollow mold beckoning to be filled, possessed, or acted upon by the three-dimensionality of another person—such is the hysteric, and such is the energumen, whose hollow personality is filled and activated by the spellbinding myth of a collective devil. Both take on our quests and everyday desires to the point of paroxysm; they both reverberate with the cry of the void, the cry of a world waiting to be born.

Every vacuum is the guidepost and focal point of a plenum. It is the axis and pivot of all that surrounds it, that is, of what is called its environment. Every crack divides the entire universe in two. Every fissure is a boundary, a mirror *between* inside and outside that *is* outside and inside at the same time; as such, it is the mediator between, and the collective imagination of, those two worlds. Opening, orifice, cavity—all point the way to the perversity and creativity that is ambivalence. They are where nowhere is located; they mark the neutral position, the point of no return where love and death become one.

The same holds for the opposite of empty space, the plenum. Every thing, be it only a little pebble, is the focal point of an empty space, a trap for infinity. Every presence is the sought-after core of a scar, a scar left by a departure, or perhaps an expected arrival that never came about.

Could the smile spreading over the white stillness of the teeth of this young woman (opposite) be a complaint about my absence? That space shall be my nest, or my grave. But first here is my variegated reply: frangipani blossoms, red hibiscus, and iridescent shells for your body—finery from the world, a whole world that is yours alone.

A Xicrin Indian of the Cayapo tribe wearing body paint. Amazonia, Brazil

Surma women from the Omo valley in Ethiopia wear monstrous artificial lips that ethnologists refer to as labrets and which have earned them the nickname of "plate women." Do they wear them to be seductive? Or, as some experts have suggested, are they trying to look like a totemic ancestor of the frogman variety? The mystery has yet to be solved. In any event, these disfiguring adornments are a good deal more cumbersome than dental plates: when one has circular wooden lips measuring ten centimeters or more in diameter, the simple act of eating becomes an acrobatic feat! The demands that the Nambicuara of Mato Grosso (Brazil) make of their female companions are not as stringent: two or three lines painted on the cheeks, and nothing—not even a loincloth—covering the body, except a vegetable dye.

Right: *Nambicuara Indians. Mato Grosso, Brazil*
Below: *Surma women. Ethiopia*

Surma woman.
Ethiopia

Here are the "cannibals," their faces coated with a mixture of grease and pigment, their brows wreathed with shells or cheap buttons imported from Europe or Hong Kong. The individuals pictured opposite and below belong to the Iwam tribe that dwells along the upper Sepik River in New Guinea. Though our contemporaries, these warriors still live in the Stone Age. In order to overcome the wild boar or bring an enemy to bay, Sepik men dress themselves up in the tusks that embody the power of their adversaries: the canine teeth of warthogs are inserted through holes made in the nasal septum, and cassowary quills are shoved through the alae of the nose. To seduce? To do battle? New Guinea warriors obtain their weapons from enemy and prey alike: teeth, feathers, and shells.

Iwam warriors. Upper Sepik River, New Guinea

Woman belonging to a Paleonegritic tribe. Nigeria ▷

Enaratoli, Irian-Barat, New Guinea

The only clothing these New Guinea mountain dwellers indulge in takes the form of penile sheaths proudly hoisted up and held in place by a cord slung about the waist. What curious G-strings these ostentatious casings make! They are reminiscent of the phallus-shaped talismans that girls and women used to wear in ancient times. And what an astonishing contrast between the nudity of these men and the rich finery worn by certain tribes that make their home in the valleys: crests fashioned of bird-of-paradise feathers, mother-of-pearl necklaces, and breastplates made from opossum fur!

Wahgi girls.
New Guinea

31

Night has fallen in the bush. Constellations of markings in the shapes of flowers and bird's feet spangle the brown bodies of the dancers (p. 32). They look as if they've been shot through with starry holes that glow from within. But now the forest itself appears on the scene in the guise of the daughter of a Papuan chief. Here she is (at left), crowned with a possum-fur headdress, her painted face concealed behind a mesh of plant fibers, her throat encased in a setting of seed necklaces, her chest sporting a giant shell. She is leading the men of her clan to a contest of prestige, during which warriors dressed as birds or foliage (below) will meet in peaceful combat.

Left: *Daughter of a Wapenamanda chief. New Guinea*
Below: *"Leaf-man." Vicinity of Kainantu, New Guinea*

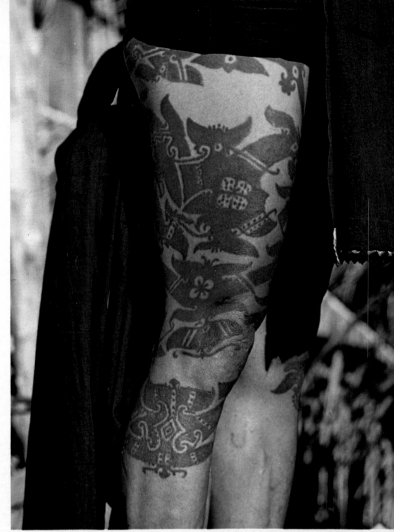

Iban tattoos. Rajang River, Sarawak, Borneo

"Tattoo" comes from the Tahitian word *tatau*. Indeed, the most skillfully executed examples of this art form can be found among Polynesians, the Dayaks of Borneo, and the Maoris of New Zealand. The technique—as straightforward in theory as it is painful in practice—consists of marking the skin with indelible designs by injecting colored matter beneath the epidermis through tiny punctures made in the outer surface of the skin. The resulting design is seen through the transparent outer skin layer; and this is why dark- or black-skinned peoples prefer the raised patterns of scarification to tattooing, which is suitable only for races with white, light, or coppery skin.

Tattoos can cover all or part of the body. Those worn by inhabitants of Samoa (p. 35) and the Marquesas are masterpieces of abstract art and might take years to execute. The most intricate specimens would be completed only in maturity, sometimes not until old age. The rules governing their composition were as well-defined as those that regulated the armorial bearings of ancient nobility. Networks of lines, hatchings, and stripes indicated rank and lineage, recalled a feat of arms, an expedition, or some other unusual event in a person's life, and specified his rank of initiation and the rights to which he was entitled. In Borneo, certain tattoos are still believed to have therapeutic value. In general, however, the socio-cultural meaning they once carried is being increasingly overridden by purely decorative considerations. Witness the elegant stylized dragons decorating the thigh and calf of a young Iban from Sarawak (above), or the honeycomb pattern on the arm and shoulder of the young Filipino woman pictured below.

Kalinga tattoos. Luzon, Philippine Islands

Sailor's tattoos. Hong Kong

In the South Seas, tattooing was a traditional art form thought to protect the wearer; but what captivated European sailors was the strange, provocative quality of the designs. In major ports the world over, professional tattooists have set up shop. Some of them are real virtuosos, as one can see by these extraordinary tattoos executed in Hong Kong (p. 36) and London (p. 37).

Neither Picasso nor the Fauves ever created paintings as savage as these! The young Papuan women pictured here are visions that are every bit as dazzling as the canvases of our great visionary artists. The painter is turned into a living canvas. These women paint their faces with shapes and colors that they have inherited from the genius of their race as well as that of nature. They are a people of emerald and scarlet birds, glossy seeds, and fluttering flowers (oh! they're giant butterflies). Gleaming red beetles are woven together to form diadems.

Their swollen breasts glisten like mother-of-pearl, and their kangaroo-fur caps are as soft and airy as orchid pollen. Foreheads, cheeks, and lips shining with palm oil have the reddish luster of blood or moistened red earth. The eyes, nose, and mouth are outlined as if to proclaim magical signs that mediate between the great phenomena of nature and the structure of man. The eyes expand to become clouds, and rain falls from them in starry blue and white rivers. A liana lattice unwinds from the forehead, over the ridge of the nose, and down to the edge of the mouth.

Women of the High Plateau. New Guinea

"Satin skin," we would say. But this young Burmese woman from Mandalay has what we would have to call "tree skin." After her bath, she concocted a beauty mask made from a base of rare tree barks ground and worked into a paste. She alone knows the secret. Her skin will be cool in summer, warm in winter, and soft the year round. She has taken special care to mark her cheeks with the delicately shaped leaf of the pipal, the tree sacred to Buddha. A woman adorned, a mirror of the world. How beautiful is the etymology of the word "cosmetic," which comes from the Greek term *cosmos:* the universe, the order of the universe.

Beauty mask. Mandalay, Burma

Left: *Navajo Indian woman. Arizona*

Below, left: *Cuna Indian woman. San Blas Islands, Panama*

Asaro tribe. New Guinea

Ceremonial body painting. Ivory Coast

A single line of makeup drawn over a thin film of paint: nothing more is needed to glorify a face or accentuate the enigmatic quality that makes it at once uninhibited and strained, open and inaccessible. In the presence of this human mask, others bow or flee. These American Indians—the Navajo of New Mexico (above, left) and the Cuna of Panama (below, left)—are as deft in

their sparing application of makeup as in their use of profuse amounts of decorative jewelry and rich fabrics. Elsewhere, in New Guinea for example (p. 42) or on the Ivory Coast (p. 43), celebrations elicit all the resources that body painting has to offer. Every individual undergoes a metamorphosis that allows him to play the role assigned to him by myth and magic.

Dakar, Senegal

Above, right: *Trobriand Islands, New Guinea*

Right: *New Year's kimono worn at the temple of Asakusa Kannon. Tokyo, Japan*

Young men of all nations, bedeck your hair with flowers. Fishermen of the Trobriand Islands, wreathe your heads with hibiscus and the prows of your canoes with curvilinear designs that simulate waves and prows of frigates. Along the axes of the waves appear the ancestors of your clan! Young brides-to-be dressed in the traditional style of Japan, separate the locks of your hair with shimadas of peach blossoms and silk ribbons. You'll honor the New Year at the sanctuary of Asakusa Kannon with kimonos and obis tied in a knot at the back.

New Year's. Japan

45

Woman of Andhra Pradesh, India

Young woman of the Chimbu tribe. New Guinea

The shaven head of this "Indian gypsy" returning from the temple of Tirupati is a token of penitence and gratitude. She is a nomad from southern India (above, left). She seems to bear no resemblance whatever to the young Chimbu from New Guinea wearing a headdress of bird's feathers (above, right), or to the little fawn-eyed Pakistani girl dressed up to attend a wedding (p. 47). However, their seemingly diverse fineries are but so many feathered and bejeweled variations on the universal theme of female seduction. For women violate the law of nature that decrees that, among butterflies, the female of the species should generally be drab in color; among mammals, lacking in defenses; or, among birds, deprived of the sumptuous feathers of the lyrebird. But the little Papuan has used those very feathers to mask herself behind the strange whiskers of some wild "cat."

Young Pakistani woman at a wedding ceremony ▷

Young Kayan woman. Sarawak, Borneo

Who would dare claim that the sole function of the ear is to harness sound? Or that canines and incisors are intended only to tear food into smaller pieces? From time immemorial, the girls of Borneo have had other ideas about these serious matters. They know that their ears are designed to hold loops whose size and weight increase with the wearer's wealth and wish to be admired. They know, too, that their teeth, crowned with gold at first, are master trumps in the game of love and chance. All this young Kayan woman need do is smile, and she reveals the emerald and ruby inlay that is her winning hand: three aces, all hearts! Pieces of jade hanging from the ears and orchids in a raven chignon prove that this beauty from Djakarta (opposite), though obviously Westernized in appearance, has not forsaken the ancestral magic of seduction.

Young woman. Djakarta, Indonesia

To seduce means to radiate a sun of blazing colors that spins round until one's mind goes blank with dizziness. A golden disk creeps up on the sun: suddenly it is night, brought on by the incestuous eclipse of the sun and the moon. The sun has been dashed to pieces; that is, it has exchanged its skin for the blood-red skin of feathered gods and has burned like a torch during a celebration held on a brutally hot day.

The "redskins" are not the only peoples to use bird feathers for decorative headdresses. Indians from the Amazon to the Arctic dress themselves up in plumes and wreathe their heads with the wing quills of fiery-colored macaws, jonquil parrots, and eagles glowing with metallic luster. Some show real expertise by crafting necklaces made of hummingbirds. The ancient Peruvians would "weave" the feathers of a bird which, like the glorious Inca himself, bedazzled the eye with yellow and scarlet. The Aztecs of Mexico believed the azure quetzal to be the incarnation of their feathered snake god.

All of these feathered ornaments carry symbolic or magical meaning, hark back to religious signs, shimmer with stars snatched from the sky. For the feather was a sign, image, and hieroglyph before it became a writing tool. It is one of the attributes of the kachina revered by the Hopi Indians of New Mexico.

Men and women representing earth, air, and water dance on the village square (p. 52). The earth will yield an abundance of corn. Clumps of feathers fill their hands and headdresses to overflowing.

Mere splendor is not enough. Adornment becomes ritual, heraldry, language. Man orders these metamorphoses "at my express wish."

The Blackfoot has turned himself into a prairie cock during mating season (pp. 54–55); he rivals the bird in beauty. Watch his headdress of porcupine quills shimmer as he dances. The large fan of feathers spread across his back ruffles like the plumage of a bird displaying himself for a mate.

Indian powwow. New Mexico

52 *Pueblo Indians, New Mexico*

Macedonia, Greece

Mogei warrior. New Guinea

Bugis bride. Celebes Island, Indonesia

Izmir, Turkey

Young Iban woman. Sarawak, Borneo

Maori youth. New Zealand

Young Toradja woman.
Celebes Island, Indonesia

Young Masai woman. Tanzania

Pueblo Indian woman. New Mexico

Overleaf: The buffalo-horn crowns and glass-bead garments worn by the "rickshaw boys" (pp. 58–59), as the pedicab drivers of Durban, South Africa, are called, remind us that they are descendants of proud Zulu warriors.

Izmir, Turkey

Lithuania, U.S.S.R.

Bulgaria

57

The most beautiful finery is not necessarily the most expensive. These Masai women from Kenya-Tanzania are wearing pectorals, necklaces, and ear ornaments made of quite ordinary materials: wooden or colored-glass pearls of different sizes. The "pearls" may simply be strung together, or strung together and then sewn into pieces of skin; the latter technique is practiced in other cultures as well, notably among Indians of the Great Plains. These women are as artful in wearing elegant decoration as they are skilled in creating it. Their finery attests to a supremely self-assured feeling for geometric decoration, to the point that one could talk in terms of a full-fledged "pearl art."

Masai women. Kenya-Tanzania

Newar bride. Katmandu, Nepal

At first glance, the finery of this young Newar bride from Katmandu, Nepal, seems to verge on the nondescript. And yet, her headband and earrings are made of gold. A cultural difference, to be sure, but a psychological one as well: the proud beauty of Kenyan women contrasts with the meditative, almost withdrawn beauty of this Nepalese.

Whether understated and delicate, or haughty and "swaggering," the ornaments of men and women alike have their styles and fashions. They can be "classic" among certain peoples or take on a baroque, even delirious appearance among others. Necklaces turn into breastplates that overshadow the very necks they are supposed to highlight. A woman becomes a showcase of gigantic jewels, for what she wears with such ostentation constitutes her fortune, her dowry. She becomes the reliquary of her own beauty, a victim of the enormous pendants and gold earrings that dazzle the face of this woman of the Peuhl tribe (p. 63). The same is true of the breastplate, nose and ear ornaments, and gold rings we see on this Panamanian Indian (p. 62).

Cuna Indian
woman.
San Blas
Islands,
Panama

Young Peuhl
woman.
Mali

62

Above left: *Bride. Morocco*

Below, left: *Muslim wedding. Pakistan*

The young Sikh bride from Bombay (p. 64 and at right) could be Scheherazade. In Pakistan as well as Morocco usually harsh Koranic law allows a woman to celebrate her wedding day by becoming a princess out of *The Thousand and One Nights.*

Sikh wedding. India

Ngaundere sultan. Cameroun, West Africa

It is the hour of light and of the gaze of others. On a village square in Cameroun, the last of the "black sultans" critically examines his clothing in a 1914-style French bamboo mirror from Dufayel's, a gift presented to him by one of his wives. Is the turban knotted properly? Is the material draped in a sufficiently imposing manner? We must not smirk at the fastidiousness of this kinglet, who rules over an ethnic group that has been converted to Islam. Is there anyone of us who does not dread that moment of truth? "Do I look my best?" young women ask themselves. "I'm not unattractive, am I?" older women wonder. "Am I in good enough shape?" muses the man who puts himself through a quarter-hour of exercises every morning. The myth of Narcissus is universal, even if we actually don't always fall in love with our own reflection. For the mirror is a corridor that leads to the realm of dreams. "How nice it would be if we could only get through into Looking-glass House! I'm sure it's got, oh! such beautiful things in it! . . . Let's pretend the glass has got all soft like gauze, so that we can get through," said Alice as she passed *Through the Looking-Glass.*

◁ *Minangkabau bride. Sumatra, Indonesia*

"Do you know, I always thought Unicorns were fabulous monsters, too? I never saw one alive before!"

"Well, now that we *have* seen each other," said the Unicorn, "if *you'll* believe in me, I'll believe in you. Is that a bargain?"

Could it be Lewis Carroll's Alice and Unicorn that we see deep in the eyes of this beautiful Batak woman? Are you a child? A flower? Could you be the one who watches over the gardens that protect the philosophers' stone? Who are you? The eternal female? What melody, what call do you and you alone hear?

Young Papuan lovers. Southern High Plateau, New Guinea

On the Southern High Plateau of New Guinea, young couples enjoy the right to spend the night before their wedding together, alone. It is their vigil of love. Only their heads are allowed to touch, and there they remain, side by side, until dawn.

Threat

Whether a smile is worn by an infant or an adult, a "savage" or a member of "civilization," it is one of the most pregnant and contradictory "words" in the universal language of the human body. For smiling bares the teeth, as does another key word in the Esperanto of gestures—laughter. Either can serve as a warning signal of imminent aggression. When a zebra curls his lips and cocks his ears, it means that he is attempting to seduce a member of his species; but when he curls his lips and *lowers* his ears, he is making a threatening gesture. Threat and seduction are antithetical, and yet how seductive a threat can sometimes be! If monkeys are shown slides of other monkeys, they react more favorably to those with a threatening appearance. Just as a little boy loves to hear a protective grownup tell the story of the Big Bad Wolf, so a little monkey learns to deal with fear by first courting spectacles of terror. Men and monkeys act the same once they've grown up, too.

The ritualized tournaments performed by gazelles and the simulated wars waged by rattlesnakes pit head against head in a contest of males that will decide beyond all question—and with no risk of being bitten—the triumph of one and the symbolic death of the other. What a real show of confidence such games are! And the ones who know how to take up the challenge of fear will know how to inspire fear in others. Gorillas and chimpanzees, for instance, thump the skin of their chests or the bark of hollow trees.

A Siamese fighting fish need only see his reflection in a mirror to put his body on battle alert. The messages of fear, like those of seduction, are conveyed by the languages of shape, color, smell, and sound. Chimpanzees howl and stamp the ground with all four paws. The robin raises its beak to expose its red throat, just as the blue-throat displays its blue feathers. A silvery shaft glides underwater, then shoots straight up: it is a male stickleback displaying its bright red belly in a war cry of color that is a prelude to biting. Another male who was violating his territory must now either retreat or prepare for action, head lowered and tail in the air. Then there are those caterpillars that turn themselves into what appear to be, at least on their scale, giant snakes.

Man, take a brush and redden the beige throat of a female finch: her female companions will immediately mistake her for a male. You therefore have the power to transform the world, for you can change its appearance as well as your own. You are the creator of your mask.

A mask, begotten like the first mask ever worn by the first men of the tribe, is about to be born. The weaver or sculptor of the mask is more often than not the one who ends up wearing it; this duty is usually handed down from father to son. It is imperative that the "womb" (a tree) be a place held in awe by all, a reference point, a spot that is fraught with forces. The gestation period and parturition take place in compliance with mandatory laws and unchanging rituals, for the new mask must be a faithful reproduction of the one begotten long ago by the primordial ancestor, or androgyne. Even the date of birth is determined by a "visitation" in the form of a telltale dream by night, a chance (that is, coincidental) meeting between a message from the bush or forest and a tribal entity. In this manner, the mask takes the place of a predecessor whose life has come full circle; it becomes that other "persona" it had been in a former existence. The "old man" is then honored and buried on the very spot at which his "son" is brought into the world as the renewed ancestor. No sooner does the ancestor's power leave the disintegrating "oldster" than it infuses the "youngster" with fresh vigor. Thus, the new mask takes shape without any break in the phylogeny of masks. The mask is dead! Long live the mask!

Masks are never actually "created," but revealed by dead ancestors to living initiates who act as intermediaries between those forbears and the tribal *body*. The mask, therefore, is sired by nothing but itself; it is its own cosmos, its own symbol. The craftsman—be he dancer or blacksmith—charged with bringing it into the world is nothing more than an obstetrician, a "midhusband," so to speak.

Although men exert a certain influence on masks by giving them a terrestrial existence, masks, in turn, are endowed by both heaven and earth with the power to influence men. The person wearing the mask, whoever he may be, is a combination "masked man" and humanized mask that reappears over and over again. He becomes both a possessor and a being possessed. His sudden appearance strikes terror into one's heart, for he is "filling in" for the absent ancestor or missing god. He is the healer and administrator of justice. The mask is the vehicle of life and death; it carries the entire history of the tribe as well as all the forces of nature. It is the focal point of ceremonies, dances, or collective rituals that do away with not only all personal boundaries, but any guilt that might accompany real or intended transgressions of the law.

By renewing the bonds that tie him to primordial unity, each individual is absorbed into the ahistorical continuity of the group. The mask is the bearer of grace as well as fear.

Though more often a game than a genuine harbinger of danger, threat is nevertheless an exorcism. For the real evil spell lies deep within the soul of every man: the wish to assert his strength. There comes a day when man, acting on his own behalf, steals the magic power of the gods. Once he possesses the gods, he shall possess men. And whose name appears on the agreement next to his own? We see it through the door of History he has just cracked open: Lucifer, the Devil, Satan.

War, be it real or simulated, has always been with us, for it is an expression of man's aggressiveness and lust for power. Every male, whether from prehistoric times or more recent civilizations, has felt it necessary to turn himself into a warrior. He draws his strength from traditions that furnish him with myths and deck him out in symbols. Witness the mask of this samurai (opposite page): it is a defensive as well as offensive weapon, for it not only protects the wearer's face but frightens his opponent. The antlers crowning the helmet symbolize *yang*, the male principle in Taoist philosophy. Chinese Taoism was a cornerstone of Zen Buddhism, one of the great inspiring forces behind the warrior aristocracy of Japan.

Warrior. Okapa, Eastern Highlands, New Guinea

Your two forbidden fruit were incest and fratricide. And yet you found your fear pleasing. We call it "defiance." And yet you found your sister pleasing. We speak of "mystique." Was your faith stronger than your incestuous desires? Was your war stronger than your criminal wishes? The branches of trees and the antlers of stags became your cross: on these were you quartered. Thus did Bovidae and Cervidae become your brothers.

You were the fork in their horns and hooves. Then your hands twisted and twisted until things and creatures were turned topsy-turvy. Your hands created the object that transformed distance into access and forked branches or antlers into arrows. You felt the need to straddle space and, in a single stretch of the arm, turn the gaze of your right eye into hand-to-hand combat.

◁ *Iwam warrior. Upper Sepik River, New Guinea*

Woe betide the Asaro children of New Guinea who venture beyond their huts at night! The Unggai devil will catch them by the legs with his gigantic claws. This evil spirit that prowls about the village is a kind of werewolf helmeted with mud and crowned with horns of sharpened bamboo. And he is not the only one of his kind to threaten the tranquility of men after the sun has set. The darkness crawls with demons, ghosts, and other formidable spirits; and it is advisable to protect oneself by lighting fires, much as one would do to keep away beasts of prey.

Asaro demon. Eastern Highlands,
New Guinea

Fantasia. *Rabat, Morocco*

The *fantasia* of North Africa is a classic spectacle that was a source of inspiration for many an Orientalist artist during the nineteenth century. The Arabic word denoting this equestrian entertainment means "display." It is therefore a real *parade* that provides *everyone* with an opportunity to show off his strength and dexterity as well as the finery (in French, *parure*) of rider and mount alike. But this parade is also a simulated, symbolic battle during which *every* man must attack in order to defend himself; he must evade—that is, *parry*—the enemy's blows. Evolutions at full gallop, shouting, shots fired into the air—everything conspires to lend this vehement charge a quality that is at once threatening and theatrical. "Horseplay," as children would say. But how can one ever know the point at which pretending stops and the game is being played for real?

There is a man inside this swollen, shapeless carapace made of a frame of plant fibers coated with clay. He is a "mudman," a member of the Asaro tribe that lives north of Goroka in New Guinea. Why is he wearing a get-up that makes him look like a rotten stump or some kind of poisonous truffle? To resemble an infernal spirit? No. This earth-caked being is getting ready to violate one of the most sacred taboos of the tribe. He is about to kill a man, that is, perform a *non-ritual murder.*

The legend goes that two brothers shared a vegetable garden. One day, while the other was away, the younger brother invited a large number of his friends to join him in consuming everything in the garden. When the older brother returned and saw what had happened, he resolved to take revenge. After covering his body with mud, he and five companions wearing similar disguises took up positions in the tall grass and there lay in wait for the younger brother. When the latter happened to pass by with his friends, the mudmen attacked and killed them all.

The Bible tells us that Cain, too, transgressed the most sacred of all taboos by slaying his brother Abel. But the fratricide could not elude the eye of God: the gaze of divine retribution hounded him to the grave. In the case of the Asaro, the murderer must bury himself symbolically, for murder is considered so odious that every non-ritual crime is tantamount to slaying a brother. Every murderer, therefore, is a sacrilegious person and, as such, is tainted with evil influences from which the community must protect itself. That is why the guilty man is obliged to put on a "murder costume." By isolating himself in his shell of mud, he assumes the appearance of the mythic fratricide. It is his very mask that unmasks his true character.

Overleaf:
The Asaro also fashion clay helmet-masks that javelin-wielding men wear in simulated combat (pp. 82–83). The gesticulations of these haunting half-mushrooms, half-astronauts are meant to recall an episode in Asaro mythology. Once, when they were besieged by an enemy, the members of the tribe managed to save themselves by resorting to a trick: they disguised themselves as ghosts by covering their bodies with ash and placing clay masks on their heads.

For a lone guilty criminal or all of the members of the threatened tribe, the same clothing of mud! What, then, is their common meaning? Perhaps the most elementary of all: disintegration of the boundary separating the self—singular or plural—from the universe, reversion to the primordial magma, to inert matter.

Murderer's mask. Valley of the Asaro, New Guinea ▷

Asaro "mudmen." New Guinea

Kainantu warrior. New Guinea

Fear and aggression: two motives that are essential to the theater of the mask. When confronted with the unknown, man tries to make himself as frightening as the spirits whose power he dreads. In New Guinea, he exorcises devils by donning the mask of "long-long" spirits with curling, blood-stained lips and by covering his head with animal bones or warthog teeth (p. 84 and at left). As a protective measure, he spreads a coat of whitewash over his face and sets it off with a white chin strap that resembles the tusks of a wild boar (above).

Opposite page: *Madman's mask. Vicinity of Kainantu, New Guinea*

Left: *Demon's mask. Vicinity of Kainantu, New Guinea*

Rogayewo dancers. Trobriand Islands, New Guinea

Durutu Perahera, Katagama Hindu

At the height of his mystical elation, the Durutu Perahera, the Hindu holy man of Katagama, pierces his cheeks with a three-pronged metal fork while dancing beneath his canopy of lights and little bells (above). Is he simply doing penance through self-inflicted mortification of the flesh? Or is this supposed to be an intentional provocation, a challenge? And if so, aimed at what invisible power? When ecstasy is achieved, he concentrates all aggressive forces within himself, only to become their object. For by striking himself, he pierces and casts out demons.

Overleaf:
Asaro warriors from Papua mount a charge of intimidation. Their bodies, coated with a paint made from a base of ash, soot, and plant dyes, are decorated with bones, ivory, and seashells.

Asaro warriors mount a charge. New Guinea

Man of the Wahgi valley. New Guinea

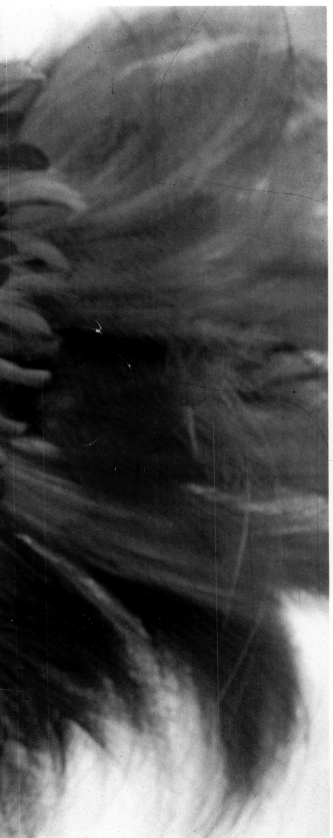

Which of these two is the "savage"? Which one would we be more afraid of meeting on a street? The Papuan who gazes at us with such pride? Or the canine head about to blindly snap at us? Who would guess that behind this werewolfish mask is an American boy from Los Angeles dressed up for Halloween, which in Europe is All Saints' Day. It is on this day that children go from house to house "trick or treating" in search of candy and gifts, threatening neighbors with reprisals if their demands are not met.

Halloween mask. United States

Wapenamanda dignitary. New Guinea

Part of the ceremonial dress worn by this Wapenamanda dignitary from New Guinea (above) is a curious "tie" made of small bamboo sticks that have been carefully strung together. If one is familiar with the code, one need only count them to know the extent of the wearer's wealth (number of pigs, amount of mother-of-pearl, etc.). But beware! If you end up his invited guest, you will be bound to repay his generosity a hundredfold under penalty of losing face. Just as war is celebration (opposite), so celebrations provide never-ending opportunities for wars of prestige between clans or other groups that are at once rivals and allies.

Wahgi warriors participating in a "Moka," or prestige contest. New Guinea

93

In Africa and Melanesia alike,
the split cowrie is one of the
traditional ingredients of
ornamental dress. (We call
them porcelain shells or
Venus's-shells.) The fact that
the shape of this gastropod is
reminiscent of a mouth or
female genitalia has made it an
especially important symbol of
fertility, just as the teeth and
tusks of mammals or fish bring
to mind masculine vigor. At
left is a wooden Bambara
mask (Mali) studded with
cowries and red-ocher
triangular ornaments
arranged in an alternating
pattern that symbolizes the
male and female principles of
life. At right is the holiday
finery of an Iwam tribesman
from New Guinea. This
masterpiece of adornment
draws on all the resources that
nature's vocabulary has to
offer: cowries, mother-of-pearl
cuttings, vegetable dyes,
seeds, teeth, and fur.

*Ntomo mask of a frightening spirit.
Ethni Bambara, Mali*

Before setting out on expeditions into the great savannahs of southern Africa, Zulu tribesmen from Natal simulate the events leading up to the capture and the kill. Dressed in leopard-skin tunics and crowned with enormous wigs and lion's manes, these dancing hunters and warriors brandish sticks whose decorative tufts of hair recall the tail of the lion. They have cleverly concealed their shields behind antelope skins. In this way, the unsuspecting game sees nothing but its reflection in false mirrors made from pieces of its own skin!

Like the Zulus, the Masai who dwell at the foot of Mt. Kilimanjaro were once lion hunters. Although their descendants still have a warlike appearance, the hunt for wild animals has taken its place among ancestral myths (pp. 98–99). The Papuan warriors who make their home on the high plateaus of New Guinea, in the vicinity of the Baiyer River, darken their faces with carbon black and decorate their chests with gigantic pearl oysters pasted onto plates of hardened resin. They appear to have stepped right out of a painting by Joan Miró (pp. 100–101).

Caste

Among bees, ants, wasps, termites, and other insect societies, tasks are distributed in a way that is as foreign to the notion of equality as the morphologies of the various castes comprising each of those societies are dissimilar. To each according to his form. Among ants, for instance, workers are distinguishable from males and queens. Naturalists use the term "caste" to designate a group of individuals that carry out the same duties.

Derived from the Portuguese word *casta* ("pure"), caste has also entered the vocabulary of ethnologists, sociologists, and historians, who apply the term to human societies both large and small. However, these experts hasten to point out that, strictly speaking, the label caste is applicable only to the class divisions that separate Indian society into four ranked groups. Be that as it may, people nowadays freely use the expression *esprit de caste* ("class consciousness") to refer in a more general way to an ideal that Célestin Bouglé defines as follows: "In order to get at an all-inclusive definition of caste systems, one must be careful not to exclude any of the three tendencies that comprise class consciousness: aversion, hierarchy, and specialization. We shall say that a society falls under the sway of a caste system when it is divided into a large number of specialized, mutually opposing groups that are hereditarily determined and hierarchically stratified. As a rule, such a system frowns upon parvenus, half-breeds, or defectors from other trades. That is, it tolerates neither shifts in rank, nor mingling of blood, nor changes in profession."

People also use the term "caste system" in reference to certain ethnic groups based on lines of descent, such as the bards (*griots*), blacksmiths, and initiation leaders of black Africa, the sculptors of Melanesia, the warriors of Pre-Columbian America,

and the merchants of medieval Europe. Let us begin by examining two notions that are crucial to any consideration of history or prehistory: exogamy and endogamy.

Textbooks tell us that primitive peoples today must obey taboos against incest as well as against fratricide. Moreover, the same peoples are obliged to respect the law of exogamy, which states that male or female members of a group may marry only those who are (a) not brothers or sisters and (b) not members of the same ethnic group. Since they are already constrained by the incest taboo, exogamy is simply a roundabout way of prohibiting endogamy. This differs from the prohibition against incest in that it concerns only marriage, whereas the latter involves all sexual relations, whether legalized by contract or not.

In the same manner, the caste system managed to impose the law of endogamy on peoples of the historical era by prohibiting exogamy, that is, choosing a spouse who does not belong to one's group. Could caste, then, have been a throwback to tightly knit tribes of primitive times? Was it a way of re-creating a collective "I" that might fill the emptiness felt by a lone "I" lost in the teeming crowd? In other words, could reversing the first taboo have been a way of recapturing the closed, confined quality of a large family? In any event, although caste came into being with History and not as the result of some philosophy or ideology, it ended up generating ideologies and philosophies of its own.

According to Vedic tradition, the body of the cosmic Primordial Man gave rise to the four great divisions of the world and society; the latter was likewise split into four separate castes.

From the mouth of the First Man emerged the Brahmans; from his arms, warriors and rulers. His thighs gave birth to merchants, cattle breeders, and farmers, all of whom inherited the prerogative of initiation and the right to wear a sacrificial crossbelt slung diagonally across the torso from the left shoulder to the right hip. The manual workers of the fourth and final class, which included craftsmen and laborers, sprang from the lowermost part of the original ancestor, the feet. It was their duty to serve others "without envy"; as a rule, they were forbidden all forms of bodily adornment.

Finally, there are those outside the four traditional castes, the ones Gandhi called "the people of God"—the outcasts known as pariahs or untouchables. Brahma, creator of the universe, your name supposedly means prayer. Might you be the symbol of a wish or appeal to transcend the fourfold caste division and recapture the unity you represent, the unity of a people as untouchable as you? Brahma, father of castes, might you be a "son of the pariahs"?

Although the caste system bristles with defenses to maintain its imperviousness to change, it could not have survived very long in its haughty isolation had it not also been a unifying force. Its mythic role is paradoxical, for its power to integrate is indissociable from the fact that it divides society into four distinct strata. Based as it is on a mystical theology of identity, the caste system presumably shuns evolution of any sort. And yet, it is an accepted sociological fact that subcastes grew in number—there were more than two hundred and fifty in Bengal alone by the end of the nineteenth century—and that this proliferation fulfilled a real human need to be identified and grouped according to one's origin, language, trade, and abilities.

In Japan or prerevolutionary France, as in India, it was the aristocracy's job to rule, yes, but to be brilliant as well. But when social function becomes caste in the strict sense of the word, adornment runs a strong risk of turning into nothing more than a distinguishing embellishment for show. Caste has the power to seduce: how could a girl be satisfied with being a shepherdess if she could not dream of marrying a king or, at the very least, a knight? However, such dreaming is not without its perils, for caste is armed with tried and true weapons of its own.

A class-conscious person makes every effort to assert himself and stand out as someone who is not only on equal footing with his peers, but *sui generis*. In a warped individual, this attitude could lead to the most terrible aberration of all—racism. Nor should class consciousness be confused with such absurd caricatures as the "castes" that people find so fashionable to talk about today, or the so-called "aristocracy" of crime. And yet, the Pudukkottai district of India was once the domain of a rajah who ruled over a people known as *kallars,* or "thieves": they would set out in gangs to rob the possessions of others so that their own princes could be adequately supplied. *Noblesse oblige,* even at the expense of honor. Order and hierarchy above all else.

This little *tulku rimpoche* (literally, "precious reincarnation") is a member of the Red Hat sect located at the Hemis monastery in the Ladakh Range of India. He is the reincarnation of a deceased man who was renowned for his great wisdom. Among the ritual objects set before him are two appurtenances that are typical of Lamaistic Buddhism: a small hand drum made of two skullcaps fastened together, and a bell (*tilpu*).

Little tulku *of the Red Hat sect. Ladakh, India* ▷

In the Temple of Kasuga. Hara, Japan

Shinto dignitary. Japan

Caste knows no age. It is determined at birth and carries with it certain obligations, such as dressing in a particular way. In ancient Japan, where the art of appearance and gesture was developed to a high degree of sophistication (tea ceremony, Nō theater, etc.), the carriage of one's head, the imperturbability of one's facial expression, and bodily deportment in general were looked upon as so many hallmarks of nobility of caste. We can already see in the face of this little "Oshigo san" raised in the Shintoistic tradition (left page) the expression he will be capable of assuming later on, when circumstances dictate. The Shinto dignitary above offers a perfect example of this impassive "mask."

The Sultan's guards on his birthday.
Jogjakarta, Java, Indonesia

Nobleman's costume from the Heian period. Nara, Japan

One wears the "perfumed hat," emblem of the Taoist faith (at left). The other wears the cap and neckerchief of the proletariat, emblems of a different kind of faith (at right). But both wear the same proud expression. The young nobleman of ancient Japan and the young Red Guard of modern China could be twin brothers. What do you see in those expressions? Faith? Regimentation? The will to power or merely the desire to live? Does the cowl make a monk of the one wearing it or the one looking at it?

Young Red Guard (Hong-Wei-Din). People's Republic of China ▷

In theory, caste systems forbid cross-breeding of any kind. Among tribal groups, however, the prohibition *against* endogamy—that is, the duty to marry outside of one's own clan—ensures an endless flow of exchanges and rivalries between human groups. Intertribal contests of prestige, notably in Melanesia, are a typical case in point, for they have a beneficial effect on the circulation of people and resources. Anything can become an excuse for dressing up, making merry, and showing off one's strength and material wealth. The object is to attract other men and women from foreign clans into the bosom of one's own community, to *ravish* them in both senses of the word—seduction and abduction. A symbolic abduction, in this case, one that is amply compensated by presents that the abductor is obliged to offer the family of the man or woman who has been "kidnapped."

In this manner, a system of exchange based on reciprocal gift-giving evolved, in America and Africa as well as in Melanesia, thereby infusing dynamism into societies that otherwise might well remain in a state of mutual isolation. This kind of system creates a network of barter and communication that is as all-inclusive as it is effective, for it links valley people with mountain dwellers, groups living along rivers with those in forests, and coastal tribes with those that make their home in the hinterlands. Women change hands, to be sure; but there are also exchanges of mother-of-pearl, provisions, techniques, beliefs, myths, and ideas. This deep-seated need is fulfilled by ritual ceremonies and celebrations that light up the collective life of primitive man and provide opportunities for full-blown love bouts between young men and women from different clans, decked out in all their finery.

Wahgi tribe. Eastern Highlands, New Guinea

Nambicuara Indian. Mato Grosso, Brazil

Masai youth. Tanzania

Daughter of a Wabag chief. New Guinea

Nias Island, Indonesia

Dignitary. Kandy, Sri Lanka

Married woman. India

Plains Indian. United States

Vishnuite Brahman. India

Village mayor. Peru

Ceremonial costume. Hawaiian Islands

Hippie. United States

Young Buddhist bonze. Himalayas, Burma

"Chief" and "head" are synonymous words. An important chief deserves a beautiful head. This Papuan chief is wearing a crescent with tribal pride. Though the sun of ancient mythologies has set, its last rays are still falling on peoples who are just entering the mainstream of History. The last kings of the Old World take on the manner of presidents, and their prefects are reluctant to wear two-pointed hats. But in newer worlds, presidents and prefects dress as splendidly as kings. Witness these two African chiefs: A diadem adorns the one pictured above, while the other wears his crown in the shade of a parasol.

Important Papuan chiefs. Gulf of Papua, New Guinea

Shinto priests. Japan

In many ancient civilizations, scholars and men of letters comprised full-fledged castes that were not far removed in rank from the priesthood and aristocracy. Since writing was often believed to be divine or mythical in origin, those versed in the art of signs were considered to be as magical and formidable as those who knew how to handle weapons. This power brought with it dignity and wisdom. During the Heian era (794–1185), which marked the golden age of ancient Japan, Shintoist priests were also scholars, calligraphers, or astute men of letters. Sumptuous costumes made of rare, embroid-

ered materials bore witness to their aristocratic tastes.

Buddhism reacted by decreeing that people shave their heads, wear wooden sandals (in particular, the *geitas* in use among the lower classes), and exchange silken robes for less pretentious apparel. However, this modesty and rigor are but a different expression of the same fundamental truth: those who watch over public records and the words of the gods are not the same as others. Regardless of outward appearance, they are always seen clasping a talisman against their chests: the book containing the Law.

Zen monk. Japan

119

These ornaments are a good deal more than mere jewels, ostentatious though they may be. Whether tokens of wealth, emblems of caste, or objects connected with religion, they are all props in the theater of worship or social interaction. In Tibet, near the Indian border, only noblewomen may wear the costly "cobra" headdress whose front part consists of a piece of material that is first cut into the shape of a snake's head, then covered with pieces of turquoise and silver plates. The back portion, which is fashioned to simulate the body of the snake, reaches down as far as the nape of the neck and is embellished with black lambswool braids and silver pendants.

Zuni Indians. New Mexico

The Zuni Indians of New Mexico are renowned gold- and silversmiths. Men and women alike blanket themselves with necklaces, pendants, and silver-and-turquoise rings for the "shalako" ceremonies, during which the people celebrate the periodic reemergence of the masked rainmaking giants from their underground abode, the tribal sanctuaries known as kivas.

The wish to "feel at home" is not that far removed from class consciousness. There was a time when nations could be distinguished by their costumes, their mode of dress; every region had its own headdresses and clothing as well as dialect and customs. One could instantly differentiate between women from Arles and Brittany, or a girl from Quimper and one from the Ile de Sein. Today, ethnic groups that have held on to traditional clothing are few and far between. The Japanese go around in jeans, as do models in Paris or students in Chicago. However, the Lapps of northern Europe still wear their national costume, which typically consists of reindeer-skin moccasins, leggings, and the *kufte,* a blue tunic gallooned with red embroidery.

Lapps. Finland, Norway, and Sweden

Shall we say "hats off" or "down with hats"? Governments are in a state of flux, and the hierarchy of caste is now being overshadowed by the class struggle. Will new castes come into being? Boundaries between words are tottering and becoming blurred. What will happen to the taboos against endogamy and exogamy? Consider, at left, members of the British gentry attending official ceremonies being held in honor of the birthday of Her Majesty Queen Elizabeth II. They are wearing top hats known as toppers or, if equipped with a spring device that enables the wearer to collapse the hat and tuck it under his arm, opera hats. They were invented by a Monsieur Gibus: just think how many rabbits were pulled out of *those* hats! At right: Soviet delegates on an official visit to Lenin's tomb in Moscow's Red Square. They prefer soft, flexible hats and heraldic crossbelts that form a "bend," unlike the sacrificial cords that Brahmans wear "bendwise sinister." Myths of the world, unite!

Overleaf:
Fortunately, innocence and beauty
are not prerogatives of caste. Sleep
contentedly in your cradle, little
papoose, baby of the Yakima tribe,
future man roaming the Great Plains.
And you, girl of Arles, dream of the
love that is coming your way from
the sea. ▷

Little Yakima
Indian papoose.
United States

Woman from
Arles, France ▷

126

Ritual

The horizon vibrated like a cord. At the zenith, a huge cloud split apart and from it streamed rainbow-colored rays of light. Whisperings filled the air. Myth was there, present, palpable. And then the one who heard the voice of the gods spoke for all mankind, and men invented a new language that put them in touch with the invisible. Just as they had created words, music, and tools, so now they established rituals, the handwriting of myths.

The thing that religion and magic have in common is ritual. Whether one looks upon it as something instituted by gods or executed by magicians, ritual provides a way for everyone to have a share in divinity. It is the law and conscience of a collective body. It is as if all of the participants acted as a body for the ritual, as if they enveloped a single skeleton with their flesh and were themselves wrapped in a single skin shimmering with their various finery. Thus, ritual is the collective medium of human thought and human flesh.

If bodily adornment is communion, then ritual is its vehicle. It is an ecstasy-inducing process, an act of magic that channels occult forces toward a particular action. Performing a ritual means opening a door to another world by carrying out gestures and uttering words that have always proved to be efficacious. Ritual disrupts chronological time: it is the eternal return, for it can transform any given moment into a new beginning. By repeating itself, yet always remaining the same, ritual provides a world in perpetual motion with a recurrent, unvarying element of security.

Among primitive peoples, who see themselves as forming a kind of "body" with the universe and who still perceive magic and religion as intermingled phenomena, the medicine man does not perform a ritual pouring of water *in order* that it might rain. Everything is done as if *he him-self* were actually raining, as if he were raining along with the sky. When the French say *il pleut,* they do not take notice of the fact that the two-sided pronoun *il* is personal as well as impersonal, a grammatical Janus.

To say that ritual marks the periodic repetition of a return to timelessness is tantamount to saying the converse, namely, that the interval between rituals allows each person's body to once again become infused with time and History. Rituals punctuate the flow of life; and it is to this beat that patiently prepared, long-awaited celebrations break out in dance.

The aim of all ritual, whether magical or religious in nature, is to throw a bridge between the two banks of a river that some call life, others, death. In any event, every river is a symbol of the time that separates this world from the hereafter. In ancient Rome, the head of the college of priests was called *Pontifex Maximus,* or "great bridge-maker," a title inherited by the Supreme Pontiff of the Christian church. The same symbolism may be found in many regions of the world. In Guinea, for example, liana bridges may not be constructed without performing certain rituals. The needed materials must be cut in the forest by initiates and woven together only after sunset. Up there, above the river, the night comes alive with shadows that move across the starry skies. There is creaking, rustling, moaning. The rising sun finds the banks of the river joined by a thread of plants. There it is. This bridge is a secret. This bridge is *the* secret.

Every crossing from one place to another, from one space to another, from the profane to the sacred, stirs up mental and emotional reverberations, fleeting impressions from daily life or from special feelings experienced during celebrations. The bridge beckons the passerby, as does the mouth of a cave, the door of a hut, or the smile of a woman. Many are the thresholds hat call out to me, and the space within me resonates in reply. Every person is a tight-rope walker, performing his life on a razor's edge that slices the universe in two. This rift creates an empty space that becomes a magnet for symbols; it hollows out a "straight gate" leading to a kingdom that man would rule by virtue of the aptly named "symbolic role" he is privileged to play. Every empty space, every orifice, tunnel, or threshold is an invitation to pass through, pursue the adventure, go beyond. That is the meaning of the first rite of passage, the rite of initiation. To be sure, modern con-ceptual thought harnessed time in order to invent "appointments"; but so-called primi-tive thought had already invented "encoun-ters," for it had conceived the notion of a hole before making it. The "concrete abstraction" of primitive man's natural en-vironment awakened his power to think symbolically. Round, iridescent pearls, polished pebbles, pointed, keen-edged flints, shells, crystals—the geometric shapes of land and sea were chosen like so many soothing stones; they were the rough sketches of those structures that he would one day externalize and make the object of lucid creation.

Focusing is a decisive act on the part of the imagination. Centers and axes desig-nate the same things as symbols and con-cepts do. They coalesce images, phenom-ena, and processes into homogeneous units of meaning. The ability to focus allows the images and emotions of individuals com-prising a single community to converge to-ward a single point that acts as both an ideodynamic source and a frame of refer-ence. With this semaphore as its criterion, the oneiric world of individuals becomes organized into a collective imagination, one that molds the archetypes to which some have attached such crucial importance.

This point of convergence and di-vergence is actually an empty space, a chink in the supremely hard, opaque barrier that limits our freedom and hinders our move-ment. It is a beam that man projects onto the universe around him. When prehistoric man made holes in inert matter or pierced animals with his stone axe, he was already projecting his power of abstraction onto the outside world. The hole was and still is the symbol of all symbols. It is the light begotten in a flash by the first flint that pierced a forehead.

Initiation of Bantu youths. Village of Xhosas, Transkei ▷

Day by day, everything I experience is refracted not only by my human, social, and geographic environment, but also by the mental imagery of what I dream while awake or asleep. On my end of this process, I amass the data of experience in psychic "centers" that store, so to speak, units of emotional energy. The intensity of these "charges" increases as each day supplies me with fresh experience, and the same is true of their magnet-like power over everything that life sends my way. Like energy-charged atoms, these centers might suddenly burst one day or choose instead to release their power a little at a time. Whatever the outcome, the end product marks a new beginning, for, from that moment on, it will have been my creation.

Whether it be a concrete object (a door or a bridge), a physical space (caves, fissures), or an object of thought (symbols, concepts, myths), every such center performs three fundamental tasks. The first is to gradually systematize the perceptual and psychic content of the imagination. The second is to increase the intensity of inner ambivalences and, consequently, of the dynamic relationship between motivations and inhibitions. The third is to stimulate the need to create or act.

Wishes are creative in that they project their own image into objects that, in turn, become the symbolic equivalents of psychic centers. This allows my wish to break free of that part of me that is purely my "self." Once translated into action, my quest for a center can lead me to enter in communion with others by participating in rituals. Granted, a ritual can end up

being exploited for purely personal ends; it can lose its meaning if reduced to a series of mechanical gestures. But before either of these occurs, ritual is a collective phenomenon.

Ritual provides us with a way of rediscovering the original, most elemental gestures; for every movement we make is but a distant ricochet of a gesture performed by the earliest men.

Why these small, round blobs of blue paint, these smoky patches of shadow that dot a skin whose freshly applied whiteness is itself only a short-lived layer of color? (See p. 131.) For my skin was black yesterday, and it shall be black again tomorrow. When a ceremony is in progress, however, it is coated with kaolin. It was once the color of a clay that is both my counterpart and my antithesis, a clay that both reflects and opposes me. In the old days, you see, these little blue spots spoke a language all their own. They had a meaning and a significance that could be deciphered like so many letters. Today it is my turn to wear them and make you aware of them. I am the messenger of my ancestors, who are your ancestors, too. The signs you see on my skin are their words. Whether you be race or caste, your boughs—large or small, plentiful or reduced to but a few limbs—shall never be the trunk of the great tree of life. You must abandon yourself to the womb of the night in order to travel the path of roots that lie beneath the ground.

So here I stand at the threshold of the grove of mysteries. I see once again the trunks of those tree ferns whose strange shapes recall modern sculpture of the nonrepresentational variety. They form a kind of

doorway on the side of the road leading down from the hillside village. Two vertical stiles joined by a lintel. These tree ferns, like those of the New Hebrides, are sculptured at the other end of the world. There, in the forests of the Guinea highlands, near Liberia, they, too, are spangled with spots, striped with yellow, blue, red-ocher, and white lines, painted with kaolin or with colored clays, metallic oxides, and plant dyes. This door is guarded by nothing but a taboo: an invisible sentry, all the more formidable! The prohibition lies within ourselves. Whoever unlawfully crosses this threshold violates holy ground and courts death. At night, when the call of Afwi, the mythical ancestor of the Tomas, is heard along this path, the men make their way down the hill in silence. Their black silhouettes carry small hurricane lamps purchased in town. They are extinguished one by one as they pass beneath the archway leading to the grove.

After the men have left their huts, the women do not say a word. They curl up in their beds. The drumlike beat of the insects falls silent. All await the echo of the moment that witnessed the creation of the world. Above the village, two roars, one as powerful as the other, are heard in succession like the panting of a giant bellows. The skies are hushed, and one would say that the earth is giving birth. Suddenly, the first cry is heard, the cry of all trees, all animals, all human beings and their ancestors.

Many are the rites of passage that require the candidate to dissolve into the darkness in order to be reborn in the light. A dummy made of woven plant fibers represents a monster that "swallows up" the adolescent to the throbbing beat of clappers. Elsewhere, the neophyte must crawl through a sort of tunnel formed by the spread legs of all the women of the tribe lined up in single file. Why this death? Why this rebirth?

It is because I am exchanging my individual birth for a collective birth. I am exchanging my mother's womb for the womb of the tribe, of Mother Nature. Open up my skin, smash this wailing "self" to pieces, turn my flesh inside out like a glove!

I am a child today, but later on I shall be a man. During the interval separating these two stages, I am going to lead a life of absence, go into exile from the village, withdraw from the huts of my mother and sisters so that I might draw nearer to the vastness of nature. I've been told that, deep in the womb of the forest, I may meet my father for the first time. I still do not know what those words mean or what secret they are trying to tell me. What I *do* know is that this passage obliges me to undergo a whole series of ordeals. Not the kind of ceremony that is repeated periodically, but a ritual that takes place only once in a lifetime and is repeated only when handed down from father to son. As for me, I'll have no further need to relive it. I'll return to my village, having learned how to handle weapons and tools and how to fish and hunt. I shall know agony and fear, but I'll know how to face them from now on. I'll have a wife and children. And when I go back to Tuveleou, where kola nuts abound, I'll be a twice-born man.

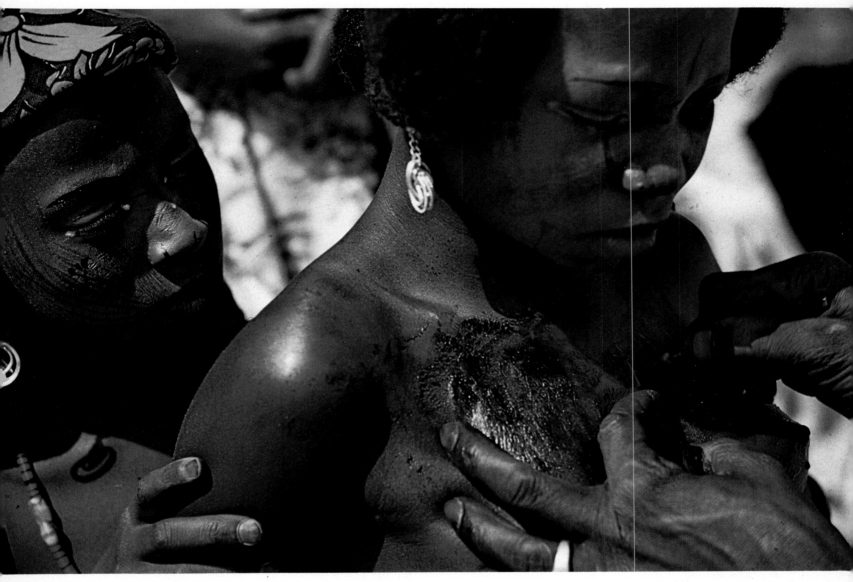

Scarifications, Kaleri tribe. Nigeria

The blood flowing from these wounds will result in raised scars that will one day be a source of co-quettishness and pride for this young Kaleri woman from Nigeria. In the meantime, however, she will have to submit to many cruel operations of this sort. The healing of the wounds must be retarded by means of irritating dressings made from a base of various plant juices and powders. Not a single groan, not a single *gesture of rebellion from the patient.* Only an im-perturbability that is scarcely belied by momentary winces of pain. Her prevailing expression is one of curiosity and detachment, as if someone else were undergoing the ordeal in her place. "From now on I shall be a daughter of the Red Negresses," she seems to be saying to herself, "and my skin shall look like theirs, and the scarifier shall chisel it as finely as the skin of chiefs and daughters of chiefs."

Ivory Coast, Gblablasso, Man area
Dance of the young initiated girls ▷

These "Red Negresses" cry out "Zaki! Zaki!" to wish you peace. Their breasts show the gracefulness of youth or the distention brought on by motherhood; their torsos are emblazoned by scarification, signs both distinctive and symbolic. Though obviously of decorative value, these stippled designs carried social meaning as well, for they indicated a woman's clan, position within her family, age group, and class. Today, decimated by hunger and lack of water, the "Red Negresses" have all but vanished from Nigeria. But ritual scarification of both men and women is still practiced in many regions of black Africa.

Scarifications, Kaleri tribe. Nigeria

Only yesterday the young initiate saw a mask heading toward him in the dazzling sunlight of the village square. It was night on the march. Today a man unmasked himself before the neophyte in the forest of mysteries: this villager may have been his own father. Although the novice can no longer be unaware of who guards and wears the mask, the secret is just as well kept as it was before. It remains intact because it is only shared. "What is involved," writes Roger Bastide, "is separating male religion from female religion, thereby distinguishing between the superimposed levels of meaning carried by mystical symbols. In short, this process takes religion from the exoteric to the esoteric." The secret is safe: is the new initiate is nothing more than a change of guard.

It is very important that the novice "take shape" on a social as well as physical level, that he not only undergo physical transformation by having marks made on his flesh, but accede to a new status, a new station. Everything is done as if the child of a single mother and a single father had to be born again, but this time from the womb of the entire tribe. That is the underlying meaning of the Hottentot custom requiring the new initiate to go to the house of his natural mother and insult her as a way of demonstrating that she has indeed become a stranger to him.

In the Ndembo or Nkita societies of the Congo, the ritual is performed in a sacred wood called the *vela*, whose boundary is marked off by multicolored pickets. Woe betide anyone who crosses it without having first been initiated! He shall be beaten, sometimes until he dies. When the given day arrives, a single novice, then two, then three collapse on the village square. The *ganga,* or initiator, takes them at once into the *vela* enclosure. According to Olof E. Briem, the exile imposed on the young men "lasts from six months to three years." During this time, the *ganga* looks after their bodies, which become reduced to bony skeletons. Then, using formulas that are part of his magic art, he gives them the flesh and blood to which they are entitled as "newborn" initiates.

Ritual excision of the clitoris is observed by only a small number of primitive peoples. Circumcision of boys, on the other hand, has been performed uninterruptedly since ancient times and is still a common practice among a wide variety of peoples of vastly different histories, cultures, and standards of living. Tattoos, scars, and other forms of mutilation are also an integral part of initiation rites. In black Africa, men and women alike bear the marks of scarification. A Guinean legend has it that these scars are the teethmarks of the great mythological ancestor, Afwi, who chews up and swallows the neophyte only to bring him forth again into the light. Elsewhere, an incisor is broken, an earlobe is cut, or a phalanx is cut off—cruel, bloody rituals, yes; but they do nothing more than mirror life itself, which is conceived in aggression and brought forth in pain. Their purpose is not only to mold a new body, but to make the neophyte suffer so that he might take shape. In many instances, adolescents are beaten with switches or, as in the case of the Indians of the Great Plains, suspended from hooks that tear at the flesh. Thus, by forcing every individual to become acquainted with suffering, terror, and agony, rituals aim at *opening up* the self so that it may bear its fruit—a new man, a new woman.

The symbolism of being "opened up" has been with us since prehistoric times. There is unmistakable evidence going back as far as the Paleolithic period: antlers from the Aurignacian and Magdalenian periods, hieroglyphs that show things being spread apart, drawings that depict quartering scenes, countless shells perforated with a hole. And then there is that Chancelade skull whose teeth were perforated during a ritual carried out some fifty thousand years ago deep in a cave in Dordogne.

Initiation is a ritual perforation. It opens up a "light" in the body and soul of the initiate, the same way anatomists speak of cavities within our bodies, or technicians refer to the port of a motor or other machine, the mouth of a musical instrument, and the bore or muzzle of a firearm. Through this aperture, the initiate gains access to the hidden side of the world, to a beyond that transcends concrete reality, to an esoteric significance that transcends patent meaning, clear-cut fact, and everything that is obvious. In so doing, the novice breaks through a wall—intangible, but impenetrable to the uninitiated nonetheless—that is finer than the silvering of a mirror and deeper than an abyss. In Guinea, this barrier was materialized in the following manner. Newly initiated boys would have to walk along the path in single file as they made their way from the forest of mysteries to the village. At a certain spot, the initiators had set up their "barrier," if it could be called that: a thin line of leaves, nothing more. One had to cross it or die. Some of them stumbled, or so it seemed.

Broken teeth, perforated teeth—eloquent, eternal symbols of the "light" that it is ritual's task to open up. The skeleton, the mineral framework of our organic tissue, is the symbol of death: life, for however long it lasts, lets only the teeth show through, to smile or devour, seduce or terrify. The teeth are where life and death intermingle. To lose teeth is to lose time, to die.

The rite of passage is a passage through death that one might be reborn as a different person, as a body that has undergone a spiritual transformation. The entire body of the novice is painted with white lines that represent the skeleton *on the surface of the skin,* and his head is shaved to look like the skull of a dead person (*see* pp. 140–41).

Paleolithic men kept skulls in their abodes; the Dayaks of Borneo—who were headhunters not so very long ago—collect them today. The skulls are still suspended above their hearths; for if they get cold, it is believed that these skulls begin to speak and interfere with the life of the clan (*see* p. 186).

Every unclothed body can still be stripped bare: one need only tear away the flesh. And so death arrives. Two holes, very round, blacker than black, gaze at us. Our living eyes do not see what is moving about in those shadowy pits. But their darkness has spoken; the door has been cracked open. And our gaze takes advantage of it by slipping into those hollow sockets and going beyond to dwell in the night.

*"Bagre" initiation ceremony of the
Lobi tribe. Upper Volta*

In Africa, the dance of the dead held within the sacred
enclosure set aside for initiation rites provides a moment
of respite. Young breasts show through the mesh of an
imaginary skeleton that has been painted on the torso of
this adolescent (p. 140). The simulated kaolin "skulls"
of the initiates are filled with youthful laughter and
amazement. Ancestors never die: here they are, they've
returned, they've come back to life. Their whitened
bones call out for new flesh, which in turn infuses the
neophyte with new life.

Overleafs:

An incarnation of the Mountain Spirit (p. 142) during
puberty rites performed by the Apache Indians of New
Mexico. ▷

A "black-headed demon" mask-costume used for
rituals involving magic medicine. Sri Lanka (p. 143). ▷

Apache
Indian.
New
Mexico

142

"Tovil," or masked exorcism dance. Sri Lanka

Kava *ceremony. Fiji Islands*

Drinking from the same cup is a rite of fellowship performed the world over. In the Fiji Islands, the *kava* ceremony is a prelude to all important gatherings. Herbs are allowed to steep in a large cup whose feet are surrounded by a cord made of coconut fibers, symbol of fellowship. Everyone then partakes of the drink after it has been filtered through hibiscus leaves.

Overleaf
Bathing is as much a playful delight as it is a ritual of
purification. To immerse oneself in the holy lake of
Kartika Purnima is to return to the ''primeval waters.''

Lustral bath. Pushkar, India ▷

The Red Hat Lamas of Tibet believe that the sound of these telescopic horns drives away demons (above). A rabbi (above, right) blows the shofar to signal the end

Gamelan players (center, right) provide the beat for sacred dances. The call of the conch announces the opening of Tantric ceremonies (below, right).

Red Hat Lamas blowing the Dung-Chen horns. Ladakh, India

Above: *Rabbi blowing a shofar. Cochin, Kerala, southern India*

Middle: *Hammer gamelans, percussion instruments.
Bali, Indonesia*

Below: *Lama blowing a t'ung. Hemis monastery, Ladakh, India*

"Beauty,"
one of the
great "roles"
of classical
Chinese
theater.

*Chinese
theater.
Singapore*

Above: Finishing touches for the costume of a Balinese dancer. *Below, left:* An actor makes himself up as Thadi, an evil character in the *Kathakali* drama of southern India. *Below, right:* A child of Mali undergoes ritual scarification.

Above: *Legong dancer. Bali*

Below, left: *Makeup of Kathakali, India*

Below, right: *"Sigui," a ritual ceremony. Dogons, Mali*

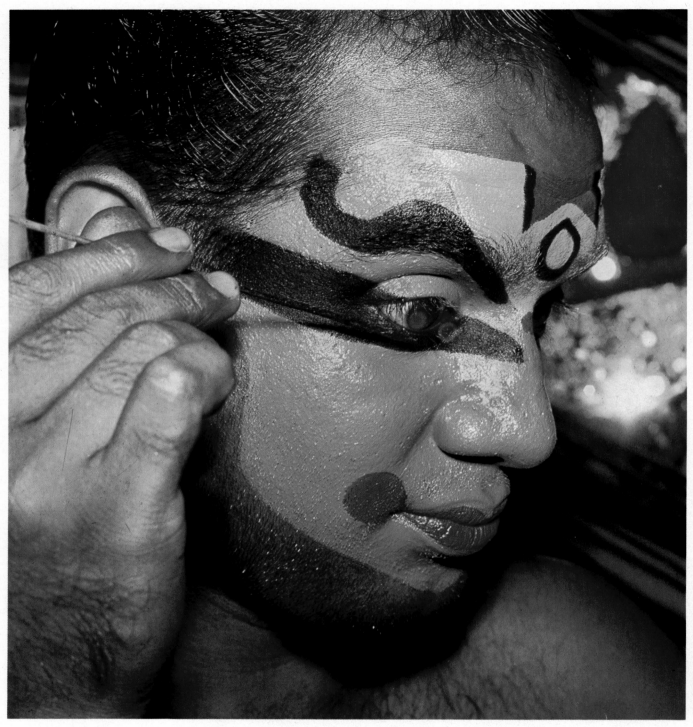

Makeup of Kathakali. Southern India

As sacredness grows less important, ritual turns into theater. But symbolic gestures and the use of makeup as a substitute mask remind us of theater's religious and magical beginnings. *Above:* The role that this actor of the Indian theater is about to perform calls for a "lotus eye." *Opposite:* A young Thai dancer in a Siamese version of the *Ramayana.*

Ramakien dancer. Thailand ▷

Pasha is one of the heroes of the traditional theater of southern India. The green color of his makeup and his large, disk-shaped headdress (*mudi*) proclaim him to be the incarnation of virtue and courage. He also wears an immense skirt that is designed to show off his talent as a mime (above) and his virtuosity as a dancer.

Left: *Kathakali, a character in the dance-mime theater of Kerala, southern India*

Middle: *Prairie-cock dance of the Great Plains Indians. United States*

Above: *Pasha, a hero of the traditional theater of southern India*

155

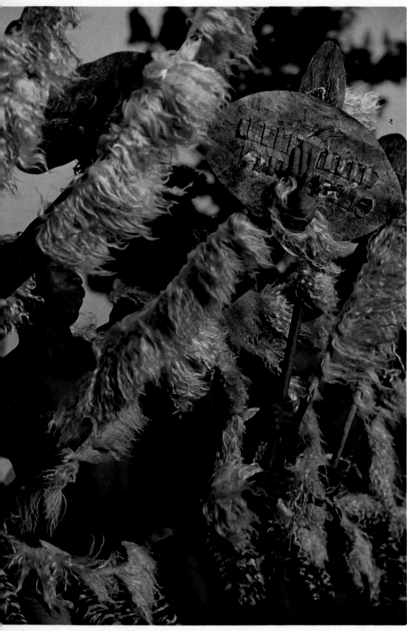

Zulu dancers. Natal, South Africa

The *Daikini* are dancer-priests of the Tantric sect, a form of Buddhism that is peculiar to Tibet. When the Law of the Perfect One merged with primitive Tibetan religion in the ninth century B.C., the result was Tantrism; this religion bears many traces of the demon worship it supplanted (magical procedures, exorcisms, ritual dances). This *Daikini* of the Ladakh Range is performing a role in a sacred ballet. He wears a brass mask with elongated ears that symbolize wisdom; the third eye in the middle of his forehead is the eye of Knowledge. His hands are folded in the ritual *mudra* gesture which symbolizes the union of the complementary male and female principles, the sun and the moon, emblematically represented by the bell *(tilpu)* in his right hand and the scepter, or *dorje* ("thunderbolt"), in his left.

Daikini *(priest-dancer).* Ladakh, India ▷

Left: *Pueblo Indians. New Mexico*

Below: *Antelope headdresses of the Bambara tribe. Mali*

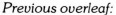

Previous overleaf:

The ceremonial paintings created by Okapa Papuans—one of the few remaining examples of mimicry between humans and insects—are a far cry from the cosmological symbolism of Tantrism. Butterflies, scarabs, and orthoptera provide the inspiration for these decorations. The designs are first painted on *tapa,* a kind of fabric made of beaten bark, then stretched over bamboo frames that the dancers set on their shoulders. Hinged pieces are added to simulate insect wings and elytra. Until recently, these "binetang" dances (from a pidgin word meaning "insect") were performed whenever clans celebrated the most important events of tribal life: births, marriages, and sacrifices of pigs.

Opposite, top left and right: Animals with horns or antlers are often associated with agrarian or funereal rituals. Horns are highly charged with meaning. For example, the fact that the stag sheds old antlers and grows new ones evokes the death and resurrection of the plant kingdom. The horns of herbivorous animals are a symbol of both virility and the powers of gestation, for they are pointed like hunting spears, yet hollow: they are both blade and sheath. *At top, left:*

Pueblo Indians dressed for the stag dance celebrating the harvest. *At top, right:* Bambara dancers from Mali wearing "antelope" headdresses for a sowing ritual; one represents a male, the other a female with her fawn.

Above and p. 160, bottom: Antelope masks worn by Dogons who belong to the Awa society from Bandiagara in Mali. The members of this secret society watch over the ancestral spirit that dwells in the masks.

161

Crested masks of Dogon country. Sanga, Mali

The spiritual meaning of masks is vanishing in their transition from disguise to costume. Ritual is being eclipsed and celebrations are degenerating into commonplace events. Thus, from these dancing "masked daughters" of the Dogon tribe with their cowrie hoods and gourd-covered breasts, to the "devils" of Carnival in Bolivia, ritual is imperceptibly sliding in the direction of purely secular theater. Parade is turning into parody. These imaginary devils, covered with pearls in the manner of Spanish madonnas, are jugglers and buffoons (p. 163). It will not be long before the mask falls into the clutches of satire: the papier-mâché heads from the Carnival in Nice (see pp. 164–65) are laughing with the set smile of clowns.

"Diablodas" dancers at Carnival time. Oruro, Bolivia

Parade of giant heads during Carnival. Nice

The *Gilles* of Belgium are the
cousins of the *Géants* of
northern France and other
jesters that are still organized
into "guilds" in accordance
with popular traditions dating
from the Middle Ages.

The city of Rio de Janeiro
falls under the spell of music
and dance during Carnival.
Although the tom-toms of the
jungle have been replaced by
drums, their beat is no less
bewitching.

◁ Gilles *during Carnival. Binche,*
Belgium

Carnival in Rio de Janeiro, Brazil ▷

Overleaf:
This young Indian woman
seems to have stepped right out
of the famous empire of the
Aztecs. She is wearing the
ceremonial dress of the Nahuatl
tribe, which consists of
pheasant plumes, a headband,
and pendants impearled with
symbolic designs. ▷

Nahuatl Indian woman. Anahuac plateau, Mexico

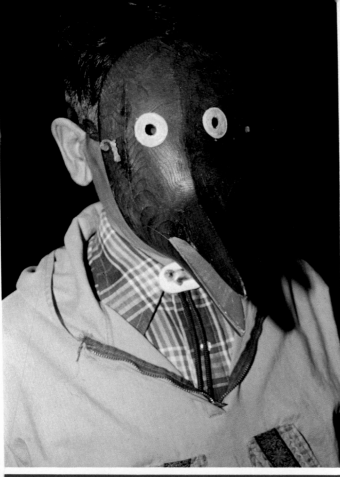

Left: *Eskimo crow mask. Alaska*

Below, left: *Eagle mask of the Pueblo Indians. New Mexico*

The sun of masks and traditional cultures is casting its final rays. But the mythical beings they embody have not completely relinquished their grip on the imagination. They continue to haunt the dreams of men, for masks are always "inhabited" to some extent and are always more than mere objects. At any moment, they can rise up again from the past to confront man with the question that casts doubt on his very existence: "Who am I?" Who is hiding behind the mask of this totemic crow wrought by Alaskan Eskimos (above, left)? What about the wearer, dressed in a shirt and jacket imported from Europe: does he himself know? To don a mask is to throw oneself into question. The eagle-nosed mask (below, left) is still asleep in the granite hills in the pueblo villages of New Mexico, but it will awaken when the hour of a new alliance between man and the universe has arrived. In the meantime, among the Bobo of Upper Volta, the "sons of Do" keep alive the ancestral pact between the spirits of the bush and the masters of fire—the blacksmiths. Their bodies covered with a fleece of plant fibers and their heads encased in buffalo masks, they go to the village brandishing digging sticks to help man plant crops and to assure a bountiful harvest through their supernatural power.

Buffalo mask of the Bobo tribe. Gurunsi, Upper Volta ▷

Maikishi hood. Zambia

Sioux Indian at a rodeo. Canada

Aardvark headdress of the Bambara tribe. Mali

Dance of the Conquistadores. Guatemala

Mask of Lucifer. Bolivia

Zuni Indian woman wearing a tablita with winged-sun motif. United States

Bird-man headdress of a Zuni Indian woman.
United States

Minangkabau woman. Sumatra

Kwakiutl nobleman. Canada

Barotse mask. Zambia

Easter hat. New York

Exorcism mask. Sri Lanka

173

Preceding pages:

A bear mask-costume used in conjunction with magical cures for illness (Sri Lanka).

The fantastic realism of this Eskimo mask representing the *inua,* or human soul, is a modern expression of ancestral beliefs (above). On the other hand, the mask-costumes of the Balinese theater, like those of Sri Lanka's "medicine men," strive to reproduce ancient models as faithfully as possible. *Left*: An actor costumed as "Head of the Monkey Army" in a Balinese version of the epic tale, the *Ramayana. Right:* Holy elephants of the cult of Shiva (southern India).

Above: *Eskimo mask. Alaska*
Left: *Representation of Hanuman. Bali*

The Pooram *held in Trichur, Kerala, India* ▷

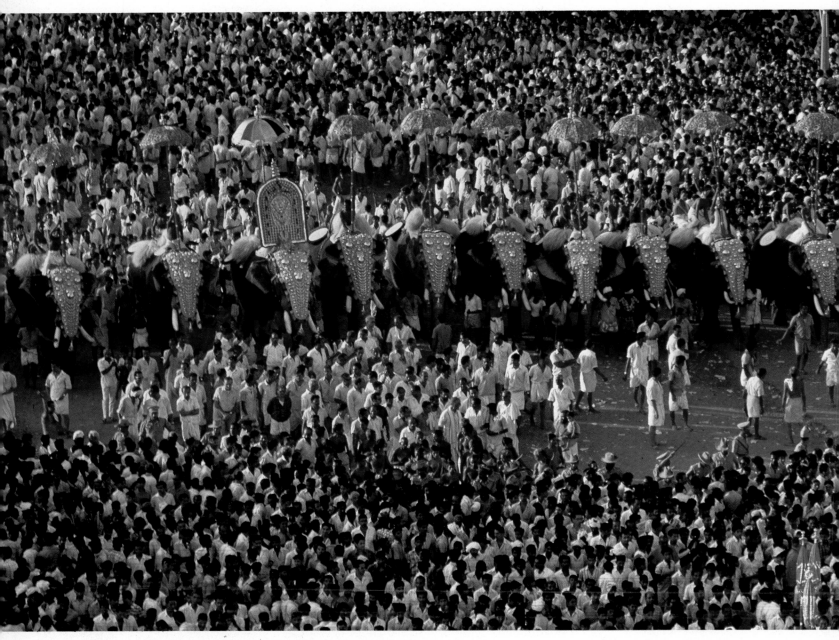

Procession of the Elephants. Trichur, Kerala, India

India, mother of gods, is the home of a complex ritualism that is as thoroughly interiorized as it is theatrical. The brilliance and solemnity of ritual ceremonies held in honor of the gods of the Brahmanic pantheon attract immense crowds whose fervor attests to one of the hallmarks of Indian life—an intimate relationship between the human and the divine. *Above:* The *Pooram,* or Procession of the Elephants, to the temple of Vadakkunatha in Kerala in southern India. The elephant in the middle bears the *kolam,* or sacred effigy of the god Shiva.

Festival of the Chariot. Madura, India

The *Rath,* or Festival of the Chariot, in Madura, Tamilnad, southern India. After the ritual commemoration of the divine union of Shiva and Parvati in the *kalyana* of the temple, statues of the god and goddess are hoisted on to this gigantic chariot, which is then pulled through the city by thousands of worshipers harnessed to the vehicle.

In Latin America, the celebration of Christian holidays assumes the tragic tone and violent colors that characterized the old pagan rituals of Pre-Columbian America. Thus, the Good Friday procession in Antigua, Guatemala, literally sets the stage for a theatrical production in which the entire population participates. The roads are decorated with multicolored designs that are made by filling in stenciled patterns with flowers. Amid the smoke of incense and copal, a fragrant resin that ancient Mexicans offered to their gods, the Christ of Merced, dressed in red and bearing a cross, is moved along the path on a huge platform carried by eighty people wearing violet as a sign of their penance. When the third hour arrives, they put on black tunics to commemorate the crucifixion and death of the Son of Man.

Good Friday processions. Antigua, Guatemala

Fire walkers. Fiji Islands

Fire is celebration at its most beautiful. Fires of villages nestled in the bush, fires of joy, fires lit for Midsummer Day. The wood crackles in the hearth, witches cackle, fairies smile, the hearts of men and women beat faster and faster, and their blood whirls round to the beat of dancing. Dance of the fire, dance of fire—dancing is the most ancient of all ecstasy-inducing techniques. At the climax of the celebration, the dancers' souls take leave of their bodies. By spinning around in a circle, the dervishes manage to escape from themselves so that they may become absorbed into their ideal, their absolute (p. 183).

Overleaf:
During cremation, offerings and sacrificial victims are consumed by fire, thereby releasing evanescent energy from the body of the deceased. Only the smoke rising from sacrifices is light enough to reach the heavens and convey the prayers of men to the gods. But the mask of death looms out from the ashes of celebration. This Tibetan dancer (p. 185) protects himself from demons by wearing a skull on his chest and an apron of bones. And the hearth of this Dayak from Borneo (p. 186) is warming a prize captured by his headhunting forbears.

Whirling dervishes. Turkey

Cremation of a bonze. Chiang Mai, Thailand.

*Dancing exorcist
wearing a black hat,
Ladakh, India*

185

Bibliography

Akoun, André. *L'Anthropologie*. Les dictionnaires du savoir moderne. Paris: Centre d'Étude et de Promotion de la Lecture, 1972.

Alexander, Hartley B. *L'Art et la philosophie des Indiens de l'Amérique du Nord.* Paris: E. Leroux, 1926.

Appia, Beatrice. "Masques de Guinée française et de Casamance d'après les dessins d'enfants noirs." *Journal de la Société des Africanistes,* 1943, pp. 153–82.

Bachelard, Gaston. "Le Masque." In *Le Droit de rêver,* pp. 201–15. Paris: Presses universitaires de France, 1970.

Bastide, Roger. "Initiation." In *Encyclopaedia Universalis,* vol. 8, pp. 1031–36. Paris: Encyclopaedia Universalis France, 1968.

Bédouin, Jean-Louis. *Les Masques.* Collection "Que sais-je?". Paris: Presses universitaires de France, 1961.

Bernolles, Jacques. *Permanence de la parure et du masque africains.* Paris: Maisonneuve et Larose, 1966.

Bettelheim, Bruno. *Les Blessures symboliques.* Paris: Payot, 1971.

Bleeker, Claas J. *Initiation.* Leiden: E. J. Brill, 1965.

Blum, Paul. *La Peau.* Collection "Que sais-je?". Paris: Presses universitaires de France, 1960.

Boas, Franz. *The Social Organization and the Secret Societies of the Kwakiutl Indians.* Washington, D. C.: Smithsonian Institution, 1897.

———. *Primitive Art.* New York: Dover Publications, 1955.

Bouglé, Célestin. *Essais sur le régime des castes.* Paris: F. Alcan, 1908.

Brelich, Angelo. "Initiation et histoire." In *Initiation* by C. J. Bleeker. Leiden: E. J. Brill, 1965.

Breton, André. "Note sur les masques à transformation de la Côte Pacifique Nord-Ouest." *Neuf,* June, 1950.

Briem, Olof E. *Les Sociétés secrètes de mystères.* Paris: Payot, 1941.

Bruno, C. *Tatoués, qui êtes-vous?* Brussels: De Feynerolles, 1970.

Buraud, Georges. *Les Masques.* Paris: Éditions du Seuil, 1948.

Caillois, Roger. "Le Masque et le vertige." In *Les Jeux et les hommes.* Paris: Gallimard, 1967.

Carroll, Lewis. *Through the Looking-Glass.* London: Macmillan, 1870.

Caruchet, William. *Tatouages et tatoués.* Paris: Tchou, 1976.

Cazeneuve, Jean. *Les Dieux dansent à Cibola.* Paris: Gallimard, 1957.

Chaleil, André. *L'Initiation: Voyage chez les derniers lamas tibétains.* Paris: Stock, 1975.

Chevalier, Jean and Gheerbrant, Alain. *Dictionnaire des symboles.* Paris: Robert Laffont, 1969.

Coomaraswamy, Ananda K. *Hinduism and Buddhism.* New York: Philosophical Library, 1943.

Cox, Harvey. *The Feast of Fools.* Cambridge, Mass.: Harvard University Press, 1969.

Descamps, Marc-Alain. "Le Nu et le vêtement." In *Encyclopédie Universitaire.* Paris, 1972.

Devereux, George. "The Psychology of Feminine Genital Bleeding." *The International Journal of Psychoanalysis,* 1950, pp. 237–57.

Dumont, Louis. *Homo hierarchicus: Essai sur le système des castes.* Paris: Gallimard, 1967.

Eibl-Eibesfeldt, Irenäus. *Ethology.* New York: Holt, Rinehart and Winston, 1970.

———. *Love and Hate.* London: Methuen, 1971.

Eliade, Mircea. *Initiation, rites, sociétés secrètes.* Paris: Gallimard, 1959.

———. *Naissances mystiques.* Paris: Gallimard, 1959.

———. *Shamanism: Archaic Techniques of Ecstasy.* New York: Bollingen Foundation, 1964.

———. "L'Initiation et le monde moderne." In *Initiation* by C. J. Bleeker. Leiden: E. J. Brill, 1965.

———. *La Nostalgie des origines.* Paris: Gallimard, 1971.

———. *Histoire des croyances et des idées religieuses.* 2 vols. Paris: Payot, 1978.

Fouchet, Max Pol. *Les Peuples nus.* Paris: Corrêa, 1953.

Graven, Jean. *L'Argot et le tatouage des criminels.* Neuchâtel: Éditions de la Baconnière, 1962.

Griaule, Marcel. *Masques Dogons.* Paris: Institut Ethnologie, 1938.

Guiart, Jean. "Les Effigies religieuses des Nouvelles-Hébrides." *Journal de la Société des Océanistes,* 5, December, 1949.

Herold, Erich. *The Art of Africa: Tribal Masks.* London: P. Hamlyn, 1967.

Himmelheber, Hans. *Les Masques africains.* Paris: Presses universitaires de France, 1960.

Holas, Bohumil. *Les Masques Kono (Haute Guinée Française): Leur rôle dans la vie religieuse et politique.* Paris: Librairie Orientaliste Paul Geuthner, 1952.

Ivanoff, Pierre. *Indonésie, archipel des Dieux.* Connaissance de l'Asie. Paris: Société Continentale d'Éditions Modernes Illustrées, 1962.

———. *Mayan Enigma.* New York: Delacorte Press, 1971.

Kjellberg, Pierre. "Le Masque nègre et ses principales physionomies." *Connaissance des Arts,* no. 139, 1963, pp. 50–63.

Krieger, Kurt and Kutscher, Gerdt. *Westafrikanische Masken.* Berlin: Museum für Völker kunde, 1960.

Kuhn, Roland. *Phénoménologie du masque.* Bruges: Brouwer, 1957.

Lacroix, Paul. *Ballets et mascarades de Cour de Henri III à Louis XIV.* 6 vols. Geneva: Slatkine Reprints, 1968.

Lapouge, Gilles. "Masques." In *Encyclopaedia Universalis,* vol. 10, pp. 588–93. Paris: Encyclopaedia Universalis France, 1971.

Lempérière, Thérèse. "Hystérie." In *Encyclopaedia Universalis,* vol. 8, pp. 686–90. Paris: Encyclopaedia Universalis France, 1968.

Leroi-Gourhan, André. *Milieu et techniques.* Paris: Albin Michel, 1945.

———. *Les Religions de la préhistoire.* Paris: Presses universitaires de France, 1964.

Lévi-Strauss, Claude. "L'Efficacité symbolique." *Revue d'histoire des religions,* January–March, 1949.

———. *Tristes tropiques.* New York: Atheneum, 1974.

———. *La Voie des masques.* 2 vols. Geneva: Skira, 1975.

Lindner, Kurt. *La Chasse préhistorique.* Paris: Payot, 1950.

Lorrain, Jean [pseud.]. *Masques et fantômes.* Paris: Union Générale d'Éditions, 1974.

McLuhan, T. C. *Pieds nus sur la terre sacrée.* Paris: Denoël, 1974.

Maes, Joseph. *Aniota-Kifwebe: Les masques des populations du Congo Belge et le matériel des rites de circoncision.* Antwerp: Éditions "De-Sikkel," 1924.

Malinowski, Bronislaw. *Crime and Custom in Savage Society.* London: K. Paul, Trench, Trubner & Co., 1926.

Malraux, André. "L'Intemporel." In *La Métamorphose des dieux,* vol. 3, pp. 254 ff. Paris: Gallimard, 1976.

Mauss, Marcel. "Le Personnage et la place de la personne." In *Sociologie et Anthropologie,* pp. 337–48. Paris: Presses universitaires de France, 1966.

————. "La Persona latine." In *Sociologie et Anthropologie,* pp. 348–62. Paris: Presses universitaires de France, 1966.

————. *Manuel d'ethnographie.* Paris: Payot, 1967.

Mayer, Adrian. *Caste and Kinship in Central India: A Village and Its Region.* London: Routledge and Kegan Paul, 1960.

Mengrelis, Thanos. "Le Sens des masques dans l'initiation Guerzé de la Guinée française." *Africa,* 12, 1952, pp. 257–63.

Minkowski, Eugène. *Vers une cosmologie.* Paris: Aubier-Montaigne, 1967.

Nerval, Gérard de. "Le Roi de Bicêtre." In *Les Illuminés.* Paris: V. Lecou, 1852.

Pasteur, Georges. *Le Mimétisme.* Collection "Que sais-je?". Paris: Presses universitaires de France, 1972.

Peuckert, Will E. *Geheim Kulte.* Heidelberg: C. Pfeffer, 1951.

Piveteau, Jean. *L'Origine de l'homme.* Paris: Hachette, 1962.

Prévert, Jacques. "Tentative de description d'un dîner de têtes à Paris-France." *Commerce,* summer, 1931. Reissued in *Paroles.* Paris: Gallimard, 1945.

Randon, Michel. *Les Arts martiaux ou l'esprit de budô.* Paris: Fernand Nathan, 1978.

Ratton, Charles. *Masques africains.* Paris: Librairie des arts décoratifs, 1930.

Rivière, Claude. "Circoncision et excision dans la Guinée Nouvelle." *Afrique littéraire et artistique,* 1971, pp. 44–51.

Robbe-Grillet, Alain. *Glissements progressifs du plaisir.* 35 m/m color film. Productions Minuit, Paris, 1973.

Saint-Simon, Comte de. *Mémoires.* Vol. 2, années 1702–1708. Bibliothèque de la Pléiade. Paris: Gallimard, 1948.

Schneider, I. L. *Masques primitifs.* Paris: Plon, 1951.

Sèchehaye, Marguerite. "La Réalisation symbolique." *La Revue suisse de psychologie et de psychologie appliquée,* supplement no. 12, 1947.

Solie, Pierre. *Médecines initiatiques.* Paris: Éditions Epi, 1976.

Strahern, Andrew and Marilyn. *Self Decoration in Mount Hagen.* London: Gerald Duckworth, 1971.

Supervielle, Jules. "L'Inconnue de la Seine." In *L'Enfant de la Haute Mer.* Paris: Gallimard, 1931.

Thévenin, René and Coze, Paul. *Moeurs et histoire des Indiens Peaux-Rouges.* Paris: Payot, 1952.

Tischner, Herbert. *L'Art de l'Océanie.* Paris: Braun, 1954.

Van Gennep, Arnold. *Les Rites de passage.* Paris: Émile Nourry, 1909.

Vercors [pseud.]. *Les Animaux dénaturés.* Paris: Albin Michel, 1952.

Villeminot, Jacques and Paule. *Coutume et moeurs des Papous.* Paris: Société continentale d'Éditions modernes illustrées, 1964.

————. *Les Seigneurs des mers du Sud.* Paris: Robert Laffont, 1967.

Virel, André. "L'Ouverture et l'initiation." *Lettres nouvelles,* no. 16, April, 1955, pp. 527–34.

———— "Psychologie et mythologie comparées." *Connaissance de l'Homme,* nos. 10–11, June–July, 1955, pp. 35–44.

————. *Histoire de notre image.* Geneva: Éditions du Mont-Blanc, 1965.

————. *Vocabulaire des psychothérapies.* Paris: Éditions Fayard, 1977.

Virel, André and Fretigny, Roger. *L'Imagerie mentale.* Geneva: Éditions du Mont-Blanc, 1968.

Virel, André; Prévert, Jacques; Verdet, André. *Le Cheval de Trois.* Paris: Éditions Le Portulan, 1946.

Wernert, Paul "Le Culte des crânes à l'époque Paléolithique." In *Histoire générale des religions,* vol. 1, pp. 53–72. Paris: Librairie Aristide Quillet, 1948.

Index

Acknowledgments

I should like to pay tribute to the men who unlocked secrets for me in the forests of African Guinea in 1953: my initiator, Zézé Sohovogui, and Voiné Koïvogui and Vego, the guardians of the Forest of Mysteries in Tuveleu, who acted as his assistants.

Jean-Louis Bédoin and I concurred in our poetic approach to his great love, primitive art. I extend to him my gratitude for his invaluable documents, criticism, and advice.

My texts are dedicated to the memory of two companions who shared my admiration for primitive monoliths: Tony Saulnier-Ciolkowski, a journalist who died while returning from assignment on Easter Island; and Pierre Ivanoff, a member of the French team that discovered the sources of the Orinoco River in 1951. On March 28, 1974, he was killed aboard his ship by pirates off Chang Island, Ranong province, Thailand.

A.V.

Photographs of Charles and Josette Lenars holding Minolta equipment.

All photographs and technical data for the accompanying texts are by Charles and Josette Lenars except for those supplied by the following agencies:

p. 131, Ph. Blum.
Explorer:
p. 26 above, 114 upper left, Ph. Marcos. p. 26 below and p. 27, Ph. F. Boizot. pp. 29, 67, 117, 134, 136-137, Ph. Fievet. p. 30, Ph. J. Valentin. p. 65 above Ph. J. Joffre. pp. 96-97, 116, Ph. Duboutin. pp. 98-99, Ph. Y. Arthus Bertrand.
Fotogram:
pp. 4, 23, Ph. Sylvain. pp. 138-139, 151 lower right, 171, 184, Ph. Dumas. p. 162, Ph. Lolliot. p. 166, Ph. F. Leclercq. p. 167, Ph. Murilo Rocha.
Magnum:
p. 70 Ph. P.J. Griffith. pp. 108-109 Ph. M. Durazzo. pp. 146-147 Ph. B. Barbey.
Rapho:
pp. 24-25, Ph. Claudia Andujar. p. 32, Ph. Paolo Curto.